LAMMA

لمة

A Journal of Libyan Studies

مجلة للدراسات الليبية

2020 #1

Edited by
Adam Benkato
Leila Tayeb
Amina Zarrugh

L A M M A
A JOURNAL OF LIBYAN STUDIES

EDITORS

Adam Benkato
University of California Berkeley

Matteo Capasso
European University Institute

Leila Tayeb
Cornell University

Amina Zarrugh
Texas Christian University

ADVISORY BOARD

Ali Ahmida
University of New England

Mia Fuller
University of California Berkeley

Zahra' Langhi
Libyan Women's Platform for Peace

Anna Baldinetti
Universita degli Studi di Perugia

Mansour El-Kikhia
University of Texas at San Antonio

Madghis Madi
Activist & Scholar

Abdul-Jawad Ben Swessi
University of Tripoli

Ines Kohl
Aktion Regen

Khaled Mattawa
University of Michigan

Igor Cherstich
University College London

Nora Lafi
Zentrum Moderner Orient

Amal Obeidi
University of Benghazi

Design by Nouri Zarrugh • *Cover image* 'Lost' *by* Tewa Barnosa

Typeset in Adobe Caslon, Times New Roman, Adobe Arabic, *and* Tifinagh–Tawalt Unicode

Translations on the following pages courtesy of Madghis Madi (Tamazight) *and* Hasan Kadano (Tebu)

Correspond with us at lammajournal@gmail.com
For submission guidelines please see our website — lammajournal.com

ISBN 978-1-953035-00-4 (print) • 978-1-953035-01-1 (ePDF)
ISSN 2642–861X (print) • 2642–8628 (online)
LCCN 2020941553 • DOI 10.21983/P3.0337.1.00

Gîrki muro meyelle ekedimîee êski kûdi ŋgurtai daha ndoŋi yê deledi yê hôkora tusa-ã yê adaga-ã yê terih nû Lîbiya du togusî čîî yêe ŋgûrtii. Ôwonni, ŋîsturu ni kûdi a koi kînjigi-î yunu budi čuwudurru kor du yêkindirie, tunda arraŋgurã kor du, tahasusa yê tira (menheja) yê kîye yê yila šiša mundu hu duna yendiri. Gunna du mura du ŋgo karaduda-ã budi duna čendudo yugonnáã ha. Yuna duna yendiriã, ndogudi di gunú ; dagi di, guru ada mura: Anturbûluji yê abi yê yili ammaa-ã (gender) yê terih-ã yê ka-ã yê edemma yê musika-ã yê karaa ndogusaa-ã yê dîn-ã yê bûrne kara-ã yê šeeše-ã yê gône kara-ã yê, mêde karaa ada ha hokindiã yê taraktuda-ã yê kayuga hundã yê. Tunda gunna du barada tira êski-todurkuda ha yê soũa yê he yibeduda ni, zaga deledii di ni, karaa istaamar-ã du bu yuna togusudaã ha su arbiduda-ã ha duna yendiri. Gîrki, kôi kôe ada gunna hoktundu ni, turo turo ho etterčinîe ni, minbar baradida-ã yê arbidida-ã yê hurgusda-ã yêe. Lîbiya du yê yuga yê gunna. Mêdi « Karaa Lîbiyaa-ã » ha zabčindu yibeyindu ni, hana-yodurkîe yiŋgal du. A gu yiŋgal du meyelle-ã čer hunã mêdi « Gîrki » di čoŋ. Ndûrtu hunã ni, hokti yê čabti yê.

«لَمّة» مجلـة أكاديميـة جديـدة تهـدف الى توفيـر منصـة حـوار لفهـم ونقـد الأفكـار المعقـدة والقيـم والتكوينـات الاجتماعيـة والتاريـخ والواقـع الملمـوس الحالـي فـي ليبيـا وبالملاحظـة و التأكيـد عـلى وجـود الحاجـة الملحّـة لمثـل هـذه المنصـة، نحـن نعطـي بقـدر الإمـكان أهميـة لمجموعـة واسـعة مـن التخصصات والمصـادر والمناهـج لاسـيما تلـك التـي فـي السـابق لاقـت إهتمامـاً قليـلاً مـن العلمـاء. وهـذا يشـمل عـلى سـبيل المثـال لا الحـصر فـي الأنثربولوجيـا، الفـن، الجنـدر، التاريـخ، اللغـات، الأدب، الموسـيقى، الأداء، الديـن، علـم الإجتمـاع، السياسـة، والدراسـات الحضاريـة، بالإضافـة الى الإهتـمام بالمواضيـع المشـتركة بـين هـذه العلـوم وتقاطعاتهـا ومجالاتهـا الفرعيـة. ونحـن مهتمـون بشـكل خـاص بنـشر البحـوث التـي تقـوم عـلى مناهـج مبتكـرة ونظريـة وأسـلوب نقـدي ضمـن الدراسـات المتعلقة بفـترة مـا بعد الإسـتعمار. «لمّة» مـكانٌ تتفاعـل و تتأثـر فيـه هـذه المجـالات و منـبرٌ للباحثـين والباحثـات، والكتّـاب، والنشـطاء مـن داخـل ليبيـا و خارجهـا لـكي يقومـوا بإعـادة تعريـف و تشـكيل مصطلـح «الدراسـات الليبيـة». ومن هـذا المنطلـق اخذت المجلة اسـمها مـن كلمة «لَمّـة» و المقصـود بهـا هـو اللقـاء والاجتـماع.

Lamma aims to provide a forum for critically understanding the complex ideas, values, social configurations, histories, and material realities in Libya. Recognizing, and insisting on, the urgent need for such a forum, we give attention to as wide a range of disciplines, sources, and approaches as possible, foregrounding especially those which have previously received less scholarly attention. This includes, but is not limited to: anthropology, art, gender, history, linguistics, literature, music, performance studies, politics, religion, and urban studies, in addition to their intersections, their subfields, the places in between, and critical, theoretical, and postcolonial approaches to them. *Lamma* is a space where these fields interact and draw from one another, and where scholars and students from inside and outside of Libya gather to redefine and reshape "Libyan Studies." We believe that access to research is not the privilege of a few but the right of all and that knowledge production should be inclusive. For these reasons the journal takes its name from the Arabic word *lamma* "a gathering."

CONTENTS

ADAM BENKATO

A Gathering

AS LIBYA STRUGGLES to shape itself in the years following uprisings that toppled a decades-long dictatorship, as the country's state and educational institutions grapple with the past and attempt to look forward, and as Libyan cultural institutions are more numerous and active than ever, students and scholars in Libya and elsewhere want to understand Libya's histories, societies, struggles, and achievements. Now, more than ever, "Libyan Studies" must broaden its horizons and re-center the means and methods of knowledge production. There is a need for a forum that does just this, while also accounting for the complex ideas, values, social configurations, histories, and material realities that constitute Libya. This journal aims to provide that forum.

Lamma: A Journal of Libyan Studies gives attention to as wide a range of disciplines, sources, and approaches as possible—especially those that have previously received less scholarly attention or have not been thought of as participating in "Libyan Studies." We intend to recenter and relocate knowledge production, aiming not only to publish research and writing that addresses new themes, foregrounds previously marginalized perspectives, and integrates new sources, but also to encourage new research interests by bringing together people whose research and writing involves Libya in some way.

The seeds that have grown into *Lamma* were sown some time ago. As students, we were frustrated by the lack of literature relating to Libya in our various fields of interest. As academics, we have been able to see the horizons of these fields and realize just how narrow they are. In Libyan writer Hisham Matar's recent book *The Return*, he laments:

> All the books on the modern history of the country could fit neatly on a couple of shelves...A Libyan hoping to glimpse something of that past must, like an intruder at a private party, enter such books in the full knowledge that most of them were not written by or for [them], and, therefore, at heart, they are accounts concerning the lives

of others, their adventures and misadventures in Libya, as
though one's country is but an opportunity for foreigners
to exorcize their demons and live out their ambitions.

Matar's image is striking—and yet, actually, exaggerated. There is
hardly a handful of general histories of modern Libya in Western
languages. The remainder of Matar's bookshelves can be filled though,
but primarily with works of political science, economics, and portraits
of Qaddafi and his policies. A few of these are valuable and based on
deep engagement with Libyan society; others are fawning accounts
of the regime as a curious sociopolitical experiment. Arabic scholarly
works published in Libya are largely inaccessible and known only to a
few specialists, but even then infrequently used. Translations of Libyan
literature into languages like English, French, and Italian have only
begun to appear in the past few years, while there are no translations of
Libyan scholarly works in Arabic. Yet since 2011, publications on Libya
have dramatically increased in number, such that one would think the
field to be experiencing a flowering. Matar is on point in recognizing
the purview of these works—by experts, for experts. Many scholars of
Libya and self-proclaimed experts, notably, do not write for Libyans.

Our goal isn't necessarily to expand those few shelves into
bookshelves and then libraries. Knowledge production on its own may
do nothing for the object of study. Rather, our concern is to provide
a critical means of knowledge production while shaping how that
knowledge is used, who is able to use it, and who participates in its
production and use.

We have often heard it said by scholars and writers that
Libya has less of interest to offer scholarship than its neighbors—an
unfortunate perspective which continues an old and well-worn colonial
trope of Libya as merely empty desert. This trope is still present in
many works on Libyan history, which view this empty space as simply
waiting to be filled by a foreign power. Our position is not only to
show that this space is not empty at all, but also to question why such a
proposition has and continues to exist. In doing so, we hope to change
the hegemony of knowledge production.

We are also aware that this journal's title implicitly adopts a
modern and problematic unit of analysis: the nation-state. This seems
inevitable, as it is an entity that is very real in the lives of Libyans and
non-Libyans, researchers, inhabitants, migrants, policy-makers, and

militaries alike. The nation-state is moreover the primary marker of identity for area studies all over the world. But we believe that the nation-state is in many ways arbitrary, and many aspects of research on "Libya" necessarily must look across political and conceptual borders. We argue that though "Libya" is our conceptual focus, it does not exist in isolation but in synergy with numerous historical and regional networks: northern and western African, Saharan, Mediterranean, Middle Eastern, and more. We are far more interested in exploring these connections and branching outwards than we are in shoring up geo-political and intellectual borders.

Moreover, "Libya" as a term and as a concept is a Western creation which arose from the resurrection of the ancient designation "Libia" by Italian colonial geographers, who saw the colonial project as one of reclaiming the ancient territory which was once Rome's. The very term, then, comes with its own particular epistemological history and struggles over ownership. We acknowledge these and take them on, hoping to trouble and problematize them in some small way.

It is also important to locate our initiative both outside of, and adjacent to, the current scene of knowledge production and publication concerning "Libyan Studies." In Western academia, there currently exist three outlets for the publication of research on Libya, all of which focus mostly on archaeology from the pre-historic to the Greco-Roman and early Islamic periods. These outlets are the following: *Libyan Studies* (published by the Society for Libyan Studies, part of the British Academy), in print since 1969 when it began life as the annual report of the British School of Archaeology in Libya; *Libia Antiqua*, the annual of the Department of Archaeology of Libya (published in Italy), primarily the outlet for various Italian-led archeological projects in Libya, which first appeared in 1964; and *Quaderni di archeologia della Libia* (also published in Italy), which goes back to 1950 but has recently appeared only about once every decade.

There are two striking things about these journals. First, their period and subject emphases work towards defining "Libyan Studies" primarily with reference to a remote past which relates to only one small part of the lives of modern Libyans. After all, a society of scholars, such as the one which publishes *Libyan Studies*, is one of the main ways in which a field of study takes shape and produces meaning in academia. Moreover, scholars working in the areas served by these journals have a relative abundance of outlets to choose from in publishing their work.

Second, none of these journals are open-access, and so their findings are only available to a limited group of people, and least of all by students, scholars, and the interested public in Libya. In the case of *Libyan Studies*, its issues are now online and can be accessed by those with a society membership or university library subscription; the other two journals have no meaningful online presence, and are more obscure and obscenely expensive. This means that there is no dedicated and specialized platform which scholars working on any and all aspects of Libya feel may be thematically relevant to publishing their research—and that the Libyans whom that research concerns, and to whom it may be very relevant, have little to no chance to read it. Any new academic platform related to Libya must address both these points.

Lamma is, therefore, broadly multi-disciplinary in its mission. Additionally, we support an alternative to the dominant paradigms of academic publishing and believe in free access to research and information. Every issue of *Lamma* will therefore be accessible online and available in print at low cost.

There is also a history of Libyan research and publication within which we situate ourselves. Not so long ago, a group of Libyan scholars in the United Kingdom endeavored to challenge the norms of knowledge production and founded an English-language journal, the *Journal of Libyan Studies*, motivated by the "need for a general forum of Libyan Studies which, while taking Libya as its regional focus, should not restrict itself to a particular field or specialty but provide a cosmopolitan meeting of minds for writers from diverse disciplines and points of view." This project unfortunately only published seven issues between 2000 and 2003 before folding, but in doing so showed that there was both room and desire for a Libyan-centered research outlet. We hope to continue the spirit of their work. In Libya, the Libyan Studies Center in Tripoli with its branches in other cities, as well as various universities, have long published academic journals (to which Western scholars have also contributed), though they are difficult to access and not widely available outside the country. Most prominent of these is probably the *Journal of Historical Studies* (مجلة البحوث التاريخية), oriented towards Libyan history in a northern African and African perspective; this, along with several other journals, have enjoyed activity since the late 1970s and early 1980s. The current conditions in Libya leave the near future of academic publishing and research support somewhat uncertain, and for that reason too we hope that *Lamma*, with access to the resources of Western universities, can also be a viable option for scholars in Libya as well as in northern Africa, the Middle East, and the Global South more generally.

Lamma is, we would like to emphasize, only one possible way in which to move toward a new kind of "Libyan Studies": one that is multidisciplinary, collaborative, multilingual, inclusive, and even radical. We believe that academics should work alongside cultural actors, social activists, and Libyan and non-Libyan students and scholars alike. This gathering therefore does not impose boundaries, but seeks to trouble them. It does not define membership but seeks to be defined by it. It is not static, but continuously changing. It does not aspire to eliteness, but desires inclusion, accessibility, and openness.

Jakob Krais

Re-Centering Libya's History: Mediterranean Bulwark, Defender of Africa, or Bridge between Continents? *

Abstract: This paper discusses Libya's geo-historical identity from the Italian colonial period until the end of the Qaddafi regime. It specifically looks at characterizations of the country as Mediterranean or African in the different periods. By examining the historiographic discourse in Italian and Arabic as well as the political aesthetics and symbolisms connected with the colonial and the Qaddafi regimes, the article shows how varying characterizations were linked to geo-political agendas. Finally, it presents a third characterization: that of Libya as a connecting link between regions and continents, which has become prominent in more recent times.

Keywords: *Italian colonialism, Qaddafi regime, Mediterranean, Africa, historiography*

DURING A VISIT TO TRIPOLI IN 1926, Italian leader Benito Mussolini called Libya "the Mediterranean bulwark" of the Fascist empire.[1] More than five and a half decades later, at the opening ceremony of the 1982 African Cup of Nations (again in Tripoli), Libyan leader Muammar Qaddafi referred to his country not only as "the northern gateway to Africa," but, beyond that, as "the defender of Africa."[2] A third depiction has ascribed to Libya the function of

---

* This paper is based on parts of my dissertation; see Jakob Krais, *Geschichte als Widerstand: Geschichtsschreibung und nation-building in Qaddāfīs Libyen* (Würzburg: Ergon, 2016), 257–412.

[1] Quoted from Pietro Silva, *Il Mediterraneo. Dall'unità di Roma all'Impero italiano* (Milan: Istituto per gli studi di politica internazionale, 1937), 491. Translations from Italian, Arabic, and French are by the author.

[2] Mu'ammar al-Qadhdhāfī, *Thawrat al-fātiḥ wa-Ifrīqiyā* (Tripoli: al-Markaz al-'ālamī li-dirāsāt wa-abḥāth al-Kitāb al-akhḍar, 1985), 95.

a bridge between continents.[3] In this paper, I will discuss these three ideas of Libya's geographical and historical identity in their respective discursive and political contexts.

Mediterranean Libya

Colonial authors saw Libya almost exclusively as a Mediterranean country with strong geographical and historical ties to Italy.[4] From the late 19th century up until the Second World War, Italian historians of the Mediterranean in general and Libya in particular stressed the predominance of their compatriots in the region, from the times of the ancient Roman *mare nostrum* to the medieval and early modern thalassocracies of Venice, Genoa, and other city-states that had broken the temporary North African preponderance:[5] by the 11th century "the central Mediterranean, previously an Arab lake, was transformed into an Italian lake," as Camillo Manfroni, the foremost naval historian of the colonial era put it.[6] The subsequent trading post empires of the Italian merchant republics were presented as precursors to the

---

[3] See also Africanus, "Geopolitica di Gheddafi: realismo travestito da stravaganza," *Limes* 2 (1994).

[4] For the sake of simplicity, I use the term "Libya" here for the territory of the modern nation-state throughout history (as do most of the authors I quote, in fact), although technically it applies to this territory only from 1934 on. For a geopolitical discussion of the colonial period see André Martel, *La Libye 1835-1990. Essai de géopolitique historique* (Paris: PUF, 1991), 84–113, 143–66.

[5] See Olga Tamburini, "'La via romana sepolta dal mare': mito del *Mare nostrum* e ricerca di un'identità nazionale," in *Mare nostrum. Percezione ottomana e mito mediterraneo in Italia all'alba del '900* ed. Stefano Trinchese (Milan: Guerini, 2010); Dominique Valérian, "Lectures italiennes de l'expansion latine dans le Maghreb médiéval (première moitié du XXᵉ siècle)," in *Maghreb-Italie. Des passeurs médiévaux à l'orientalisme moderne (XIIIᵉ - milieu XXᵉ siècle)*, ed. Benoît Grévin (Rome: École française de Rome, 2010).

[6] Camillo Manfroni, *L'Italia nelle vicende marinare della Tripolitania* (Intra: Airoldi, 1935), 27. This work has also been translated into Arabic as *Iṭāliyā fī al-aḥdāth al-baḥriyya al-ṭarābulusiyya* (Tripoli: Markaz dirāsat jihād al-lībiyyīn ḍidda al-ghazw al-īṭālī, 1988).

modern European expansion all over the world.[7] As for Libya, it was, in Manfroni's eyes, Italy's first possession in North Africa—already at the time of the Norman King Roger II of Sicily around 1150: "Tripoli would be the first *Latin* (I could even say Italian, as the Normans were by then almost totally Italianized) colony on the African coast."[8]

15

In the supposedly perennial clash of Christians and Muslims over the Mediterranean, Italian authors perceived often even the Frankish crusaders of the 12th and 13th centuries or the Spanish armadas vying for power with the Ottomans in the 16th century as depending almost entirely on the skill of "Italian" sailors.[9] The last period acquired special importance, insofar as it witnessed four decades of European control over the Libyan coast, beginning with the landing of Spanish troops in 1510. For Italian colonialist writers, Tripoli under the rule of Spain (and then the Order of Saint John after 1530) was actually a dependency of Sicily:[10]

> The Tripoli campaign [...] was, hence, not so much a consequence of the general movement that originated in Spain, but rather of the old but always renewed question of the security of Sicily [...]. The campaign was done, it is true, under the banner of Spain and the command of Spanish captains: but it was primarily the work of

---

[7] See e.g. Camillo Manfroni, *I colonizzatori italiani durante il Medio Evo e il Rinascimento*, vol. II: *Dal secolo XIV al XVI - Con un'appendice sulle vicende delle colonie veneziane fino al secolo XVIII* (Rome: Libreria dello Stato, 1934), 212; Roberto S. Lopez, *Storia delle colonie genovesi nel Mediterraneo* (Genoa: Marietti, 1997), 40–59 (originally published in 1938); Silva, *Il Mediterraneo*, 133–39.

[8] Camillo Manfroni, *I colonizzatori italiani*, vol. I: *Dal secolo XI al XIII*, 285.

[9] See Camillo Manfroni, *Storia della marina italiana*, vol. I: *Dalle invasioni barbariche al trattato di Ninfeo (anni di C. 400-1261)* (Milan: Periodici Scientifici, 1970), 85–115, 159–65 (first published in 1899); Manfroni, *I colonizzatori vol. II*, 28–69, 110–42; Silva, *Il Mediterraneo*, 93–101, 128; Lopez, *Storia delle colonie genovesi*, 68–69.

[10] See e.g. Giuseppe La Mantia, "La Sicilia ed il suo dominio nell'Africa settentrionale dal secolo XI al XVI," *Archivio storico siciliano* 44 (1922), 215–28; Ettore Rossi, *Il dominio degli Spagnoli e dei Cavalieri di Malta a Tripoli (1510-1551). Con appendice di documenti dell'archivio dell'Ordine a Malta* (Intra: Airoldi, 1937), 21–33.

Italian, or more precisely Sicilian, sailors. The base of the operation was Syracuse; food, weapons, ammunition were collected in Sicily; the viceroy of Sicily was supervising the campaign's preparation.[11]

Like this, in Manfroni's words, Tripoli became a "rampart" (*antemurale*) for Sicily[12]—just as the "Mediterranean bulwark" (*baluardo mediterraneo*) Libya guarded Sicily, the "center" of the Fascist empire, for Mussolini.[13] Another author derived from history and geography a natural right for Italy's biggest island, that formed "almost a bridge between the two immense continents" of Europe and Africa, to expand towards the southern shores of the Mediterranean: "To Sicily thus appertained, by virtue of natural contiguity, the dominion over the North African regions, which the still numerous and constant emigration of Sicilians and Maltese to the opposite shores of Africa proves indisputably."[14]

It was only a small step from such historical analyses to the political advocacy of a renewed Italian empire, of which Libya would be the cornerstone. The prominent historian Gioacchino Volpe—originally a medievalist, he eventually ventured into contemporary history with works on the Fascist movement and the invasion of Libya in 1911-12—spoke explicitly about "collecting the Venetian and Genoese heritage" in the Mediterranean for modern Italy.[15] In the large settlement campaigns of 1938-39 which brought tens of thousands of Italian colonists to Libya, Venice, Genoa, and Messina were, in fact, the main points of departure, while Venetians and Sicilians provided for the majority of agricultural settlers.[16]

---

[11]   Manfroni, *L'Italia*, 59.

[12]   Camillo Manfroni, *Storia della marina italiana*, vol. III: *Dalla caduta di Costantinopoli alla battaglia di Lepanto* (Milan: Periodici Scientifici, 1970), 290 (first published in 1897).

[13]   Silva, *Il Mediterraneo*, 490–91.

[14]   La Mantia, "La Sicilia," 233, 246–47.

[15]   Gioacchino Volpe, *Italia moderna*, vol. I: *1815-1898* (Florence: Sansoni, 1958), 66.

[16]   Federico Cresti, *Non desiderare la terra d'altri. La colonizzazione italiana in Libia* (Rome: Carocci, 2011), 179–214.

It is noteworthy that Mussolini put Sicily and Libya at the center of the Fascist empire, thereby focusing, regardless of actual geography, exclusively on the Mediterranean. Although the Italian dictator proclaimed the new "Roman" empire only following the conquest of Ethiopia in 1936,[17] the Mediterranean dimension, particularly Libya, remained in many respects more important than Italian East Africa (*Africa orientale italiana*, AOI, consisting of Eritrea, Somalia, and Ethiopia) in the Fascist imperialist imaginary. Already in 1885 Foreign Minister Pasquale Stanislao Mancini had defended the occupation of Italy's first colony at Massawa on the Red Sea as the basis for a strong position in the Mediterranean—the actual concern of Italian imperialists, for whom East Africa was a mere sideshow.[18] Symbolically, colonial planners, administrators, and experts often highlighted the Mediterranean commonalities between Italy and Libya (whereas in the case of AOI alterity dominated the image): archeologists were excavating Roman remains in Libya at the same time that ancient buildings were being restored in Rome itself.[19] Architects argued that structures in Libya formed part of the same Mediterranean artistic tradition prevalent in Italy, which ultimately derived from Roman models.[20] In contrast to the French Maghrib, Italians did not use the Arabic term *medina* to designate the walled Arab towns of Libya, but just called them "old town" (*città vecchia*) like in Italy, so familiar could they look to a Sicilian settler.[21] Even the

17

[17] See Angelo Del Boca, "L'Impero," in *I luoghi della memoria. Simboli e miti dell'Italia unita* ed. Mario Isnenghi (Rome: Laterza, 1996); Emilio Gentile, "6 maggio 1936. L'Impero torna a Roma," in *I giorni di Roma. Nove grandi storici raccontano nove giornate cruciali per la storia di Roma e del mondo*, ed. Andrea Carandini et al. (Rome: Laterza, 2007).

[18] See Mia Fuller, *Moderns Abroad: Architecture, Cities and Italian Imperialism* (Abingdon: Routledge, 2010), 44.

[19] See e.g. Pietro Romanelli, *Vestigia del passato (monumenti e scavi)* (Rome: Ministero delle Colonie, Ufficio studi e propaganda, 1930). In this overview of Italian colonial archeology only one sixth is devoted to the east African colonies, while the rest presents projects in Libya.

[20] See Carlo Emilio Rava, "Di un'architettura coloniale moderna - Parte prima," *Domus* 4/5 (1931).

[21] See Mia Fuller, "Preservation and Self-Absorption: Italian Colonisation and the Walled City of Tripoli, Libya," *The Journal of North African Studies*

conflictual tribal society described by ethnographers was sometimes likened to the medieval and early modern Italian city-states with their permanent feuds between competing families.[22]

The shared Roman past, which extensive archeological activities made visible for everyone, helped underline the notion of a renewed Mediterranean empire under Italian domination. As the geographer Paolo Vinassa de Regny put it shortly after the war of 1911-12 in a book on Libya: "The dams, the cisterns, the wells, the forts, the castles, the cities, the towns, the fortified farmsteads, the military limes, all that demonstrates the importance and success of the Latin colonization. And that we must and can remake."[23] Already a legitimation for the original conquest, this idea of a continuity between the Roman Empire and Italian colonialism became even more pronounced during the Fascist period:[24] "Italians' colonization of Libya was justified as a return; they were merely taking back what was already theirs. […] Thus Libya was not only seen as a territorial extension of Italy—as it would become officially in 1939—but also as an extension back into Italy's own past."[25] Especially during the tenure of Italo Balbo, the first governor of the united colony of Libya from 1934 to 1940, the Roman Empire,

---

5/4 (2000), 134–36.

[22] See François Dumasy, "L'autre et soi même. Les usages du passé médiéval dans la Libye coloniale au miroir de la construction nationale italienne," in *Maghreb-Italie. Des passeurs médiévaux à l'orientalisme moderne (XIIIᵉ - milieu XXᵉ siècle)*, ed. Benoît Grévin (Rome: École française de Rome, 2010); Brian L. McLaren, *Architecture and Tourism in Italian Colonial Libya: An Ambivalent Modernism* (Seattle: University of Washington Press, 2006), 105–56; Fuller, *Moderns Abroad*, 50–54, 115–20.

[23] Paolo Vinassa de Regny, *Libya Italica. Terreni ed acque, vita e colture della nuova colonia* (Milan: Hoepli, 1913), 197.

[24] See Stefan Altekamp, *Rückkehr nach Afrika. Italienische Kolonialarchäologie in Libyen 1911-1943* (Cologne: Böhlau, 2000); Massimiliano Munzi, *L'epica del ritorno. Archeologia e politica nella Tripolitania italiana* (Rome: L'Erma di Bretschneider, 2001); David J. Mattingly, *Imperialism, Power, and Identity: Experiencing the Roman Empire* (Princeton: Princeton University Press, 2011), 43–73. The most important work on Libya's Roman history from the colonial period is Antonio Merighi, *La Tripolitania antica. Dalle origini alla invasione degli arabi* (Verbania: Airoldi, 1940).

[25] Fuller, *Moderns Abroad*, 49.

understood as a harmonious Mediterranean community, served as a propagandistic model for the supposedly benevolent and philo-Islamic colonial administration.[26] During this period, archeologists restored the Roman ruins of Leptis Magna, the home of Septimius Severus, and erected a statue to this first Roman emperor of African origin in Tripoli's city center.[27] When he visited Libya in 1937, Mussolini not only went to see Leptis and other excavation sites, but also proclaimed himself the "protector of Islam," assuming somehow the garb of a new ecumenical Mediterranean emperor.[28]

But the suggestive imagery of the medieval seafaring states was not lost, either, on Italian colonialists in their search for historical legitimacy and symbolism. Starting in the 1920s with the governorship of Giuseppe Volpi—a native Venetian, who liked to present himself as continuing the Mediterranean vocation of the old republic of the doges[29]—Tripoli saw a period of large-scale urban remodeling.[30] Many of the new buildings constructed from now on displayed historicizing aesthetics to link Libya to an imagined Mediterranean past: the governor's palace in typically Sicilian Moorish-Norman style or the neo-Romanesque cathedral evoked Palermo, while the relief of Saint George with which the formerly Spanish fort in Tripoli harbor was adorned made reference to Genoa.[31] Corso Sicilia, Tripoli's new main

---

[26] On Balbo see Claudio G. Segrè, *Italo Balbo: A Fascist Life* (Berkeley: University of California Press, 1990).

[27] The standard English-language reference on Septimius Severus is still Anthony R. Birley, *The African Emperor: Septimius Severus* (London: Batsford, 1988). For a Libyan perspective see Mohammed Taher Jerary, "Septimius Severus: The Roman Emperor, 193-211 AD," *Africa* 63/2 (2008).

[28] See the official illustrated volume *Il Duce in Libia* (Milan: Arnoldo Mondadori, 1937). For an analysis of the visit cf. also John Wright *The Emergence of Libya: Selected Historical Essays* (London: Silphium Press/The Society for Libyan Studies, 2008), 302–11.

[29] See Giuseppe Volpi di Misurata, *La Repubblica di Venezia e i suoi ambasciatori. Lezione tenuta alla R. Università Italiana di Perugia per Stranieri il 21 Settembre 1927* (Milan: Arnoldo Mondadori, 1928).

[30] On Volpi see Sergio Romano, *Giuseppe Volpi. Industria e finanza tra Giolitti e Mussolini* (Milan: Bompiani, 1979).

[31] See McLaren, *Architecture and Tourism*, 20–41, 165–66; Fuller, *Moderns*

street, actually led into the direction of Sicily, ending in two squares which opened towards the sea. The second of these squares, Piazza Castello (at the waterfront adjacent to the fort), was actually conceived as the southern counterpart to Piazza San Marco in Venice, as Krystyna von Henneberg has convincingly argued.[32]

Colonial discourse and symbolic politics anchored Libya, through all these historical and geographical convergences, firmly in the Mediterranean (and tied it equally firmly to Italy). The famous nationalist poet Gabriele D'Annunzio had encapsulated this imaginary already in 1911, when he first described Libya as Italy's "fourth shore" (*quarta sponda*, beside the Tyrrhenian, Ionian, and Adriatic ones)—a designation that became a topos in colonialist writings and beyond ever since.[33] To complete the merging, in 1939 the coastal parts of the North African colony became formally an integral part of the Kingdom of Italy as a regular region, consisting of the four new provinces of Tripoli, Misurata, Bengasi, and Derna.[34] Now, Libya was "separated from Italy only by the Mediterranean, just as the two parts of Rome are separated by the Tiber."[35]

African Libya

A consequence of the colonial authors' focus on the Mediterranean

---

Abroad, 151–70; see also Salvatore Aurigemma, "Il Castello di Tripoli di Barberia," in *La rinascita della Tripolitania. Memorie e studi sui quattro anni di governo del Conte Giuseppe Volpi di Misurata* ed. Alessandro Piccioli (Milan: Arnoldo Mondadori, 1926), 535–63.

[32] See Krystyna von Henneberg, "Tripoli: Piazza Castello and the Making of a Fascist Colonial Capital," in *Streets: Critical Perspectives on Public Space* ed. Zeynep Çelik, Diane Favro and Richard Ingersoll (Berkeley: University of California Press, 1996).

[33] The term appears in his *Canzone di Mario Bianco*, originally published in the Milan daily *Il Corriere della Sera* on the occasion of Italy's invasion of Libya: Gabriele D'Annunzio, *Laudi del cielo del mare della terra e degli eroi* (Milan: Treves, 1912), 156. On the context see also Wright, *The Emergence of Libya*, 238–66.

[34] See Cresti, *Non desiderare la terra d'altri*, 159–78.

[35] Quoted from Africanus, "Geopolitica di Gheddafi," 117.

dimension of Libya's history was their all but total neglect of the country's Saharan and African connections. The naval historian Manfroni, for instance, mentioned trans-Saharan trade through Tripoli briefly, just to add that eventual trade agreements between Libyan port cities and Italian merchants looking for commodities from central Africa were more or less worthless: "But these agreements, if they existed, were short-lived because the almost continuous war with the tribes of the interior interrupted exchange with the Fezzan and the tropical region, thereby preventing the Christian ships from regularly purchasing valuable goods, such as ivory, ostrich feathers, and gold dust."[36] Although writers sometimes alluded to the travels of 19th-century explorers from Libya into the African interior,[37] the geographer Vinassa de Regny still stated that some parts of the new colony, such as the Kufra oasis, were among the points "least known in the whole of Africa."[38] As the terminology of Libya as a "bulwark" and "rampart" suggests, the Sahara was often perceived as insurmountable, separating a Mediterranean world that included southern Europe and North Africa from the rest of the "dark" continent. Fernand Braudel, the great French historian of the Mediterranean, saw Libya—even its Mediterranean part—as a barrier not only between North and South but also between East and West, comparing the sea between Italy and Libya to a liquid desert: "The Ionian Sea is the largest of these hostile areas, prolonging over the sea the desert of Libya and thus creating a double zone of emptiness, maritime and continental, separating East from West."[39]

Contrary to this image of their country as a barrier, Libyan historians of the post-colonial era have stressed the African context.[40] Where colonial authors neglected the great desert as a seemingly

21

---

[36] Manfroni, *L'Italia*, 84.

[37] On these explorers see Wright, *The Emergence of Libya*, 48–61, 93–97.

[38] Vinassa de Regny, *Libya Italica*, 67.

[39] Fernand Braudel, *The Mediterranean and the Mediterranean World in the Age of Philip II* (New York: Harper & Row, 1972), 133.

[40] See e.g. Muḥammad al-Ṭāhir al-Jarārī, "al-Irth al-tārīkhī lil-ṣilāt al-'arabi-yya al-ifrīqiyya - Lībyā numūdhajan," *Majallat al-buḥūth al-tārīkhiyya* 26/1 (2004).

inhospitable wasteland, Libyan writers have put much emphasis on Saharan connectivity,[41] a phenomenon that has led even a post-Braudelian historian of the Mediterranean like David Abulafia to reevaluate the Sahara and its "shores" (*sawāḥil*) as a space equivalent to the sea which links Europe to North Africa and the Middle East.[42] In a curious parallel to Italian authors' concerns with Mediterranean merchant communities, Libyan historians now dealt specifically with trading networks that stretched from the ports of Tripoli or Benghazi and the oases of Ghadames, the Fezzan, or Kufra to Lake Chad, the Niger, and the Senegal. Just like Italy (after Antiquity), Libya has never been the center of an actual political empire—as, for example, Egypt or Morocco have, with their respective military expansions into the Sudan. Instead, just as with the medieval Venetians or Genoese, it was, above all, merchants from present-day Libya who brought goods, technology, and culture to sub-Saharan Africa. The historian Idrīs al-Ḥurayr claimed that already the Ibadi imamate founded by Ibn Rustam in 777 AD had created a unified space for trade and the spread of Islam, which stretched "from Tripoli to the Takrur (Senegal) region."[43] According to Limyā' Sharaf al-Dīn, Libya was an important commercial hub from the early Arab-Islamic period until Ottoman times, not only as a

[41] See e.g. Aḥmad Ilyās Ḥusayn, "Ṭuruq al-tijāra fī al-juz' al-sharqī min al-Ṣaḥrā' al-kubrā," in *al-Ṣaḥrā' al-kubrā: Kitāb tidhkārī yataḍamman dirāsāt mutarjama wa-aṣliyya ṣadara bi-munāsabat in'iqād al-nadwa al-'ilmiyya al-'ālamiyya lil-tijāra 'abra al-Ṣaḥrā', Ṭarābulus min 2-4 uktūbar 1979*, ed. 'Imād al-Dīn Ghanim (Tripoli: Markaz buḥūth wa-dirāsāt al-jihād al-lībī, 1979).

[42] See David Abulafia, "Mediterraneans," in *Rethinking the Mediterranean*, ed. William V. Harris (Oxford: Oxford University Press, 2005), 75. From the growing literature on Saharan connectivity see also Ralph A. Austen, *Trans-Saharan Africa in World History* (New York: Oxford University Press, 2005); Ali Abdullatif Ahmida, ed., *Bridges across the Sahara: Social, Economic and Cultural Impact of the Trans-Sahara Trade during the 19th and 20th Centuries* (Newcastle: Cambridge Scholars, 2011); James McDougall, "Frontiers, Borderlands, and Saharan/World History," in *Saharan Frontiers: Space and Mobility in Northwest Africa*, ed. James McDougall & Judith Scheele (Bloomington: Indiana University Press, 2012).

[43] Idrīs Ṣāliḥ al-Ḥurayr, "al-'Alāqāt al-iqtiṣādiyya wal-thaqāfiyya bayna al-dawla al-rustamiyya wa-buldān janūb al-Ṣaḥrā' al-kubrā wa-atharuhā fī nashar al-islām hunāk," *Majallat al-buḥūth al-tārīkhiyya* 5/1 (1983), 85.

transit route, but equally as an importer of raw materials that were then further processed and as an exporter of own agricultural and artisanal produce to the South.[44] Other authors emphasize the role of "Libyan" traders in the political, social, and cultural life of sub-Saharan states: Ghadamsi merchants, for instance, had not only their own quarter, or "colony" (*jāliya*), in a major Sudanic center like Timbuktu, they were also influential at courts from Songhai to Wadai where they promoted the Islamic religion alongside new fiscal and administrative methods.[45] Ḥurayr presented the impact of these trading networks reaching south from what is now Libya as having ushered in a completely new era in African history:

23

> The most important results of these economic, political, and cultural connections between the Maghreb and the peoples and countries south of the Sahara were, from the Arab conquest on, the spread of Islam and Islamic civilization on a scale that led finally to the establishment of Islamic states and empires, such as Ghana, Mali, Songhai, and Kanem-Bornu. These states then, in turn, spread Islam among African peoples and there developed centers of Islamic learning in many towns, the most important being Timbuktu and Kano, where Islamic institutions and mosques sprang up.[46]

The Mediterranean community, ultimately derived from the Roman Empire, which Italian authors from the colonial era had posited, gave way in the writings of Libyan historians from the Qaddafi period to a vast African space united by the Islamic faith. Where colonialists

---

[44] See Limyā' Sharaf al-Dīn, "Tijārat Ṭarābulus ma'a bilād mā warā'a al-Ṣaḥrā' fī al-'aṣr al-wasīṭ," *Majallat al-buḥūth al-tārīkhiyya* 23/2 (2001).

[45] See e.g. Aḥmad al-Faytūrī, "al-Jāliyāt al-'arabiyya al-mubakkira fī bilād al-Sūdān: Dirāsa awwaliyya wa-ba'ḍ al-mulāḥaẓāt," *Majallat al-buḥūth al-tārīkhiyya*, 3/2 (1981); 'Abd al-Mawla Ṣāliḥ al-Ḥurayr, "al-Islām wa-atharuhu 'alā al-taṭawwurāt al-siyāsiyya wal-fikriyya wal-iqtiṣādiyya fī Ifrīqiyā janūb al-Ṣaḥrā'," *Majallat al-buḥūth al-tārīkhiyya* 11/1 (1989). On Ghadamsi traders, in particular, see also Ulrich Haarmann, "The Dead Ostrich: Life and Trade in Ghadames (Libya) in the Nineteenth Century," *Die Welt des Islams* 38/1 (1998).

[46] Ḥurayr, "al-'Alāqāt al-iqtiṣādiyya wal-thaqāfiyya," 87.

had tried to incorporate Mediterranean Libya into Italy, now the commonalities between the Saharan regions and peoples of Libya and its southern neighbors moved to the core of the country's geo-historical identity. From the 1970s on, the regime also tried to develop the desert territories with ambitious urbanization and irrigation schemes, thus shifting the country's center of gravity from the densely populated coastal regions to the south.[47] Through this southward orientation, Libya claimed in some ways the heritage of the trans-Saharan networks of the Sanusiyya brotherhood, which had dominated the regions from the Cyrenaican mountains and the Libyan Desert down to Lake Chad and into the present-day Republic of Sudan during the 19th and early 20th century[48]—although the role of this Sufi brotherhood was usually marginalized in Qaddafi-era historiography:[49] "At the heart of the unitary Sahel-Saharan mystique, taken up by Colonel Qaddafi today, is the old desire to integrate the area of spatial extension of the Sanusiyya, which is constitutive for Libyan identity, even if the Leader cannot explicitly pick up the Sanusi legacy for himself, of which King Idris (whom he ousted in 1969) was the heir."[50]

Especially pertinent was the case of Chad, with authors stressing the strong ties of Tubu, Kel Tamasheq (Tuareg) and Arab populations across the border as well as the shared history of anti-colonial resistance in the early 20th century.[51] Again, it is evident

---

[47] See Olivier Pliez, *Villes du Sahara. Urbanisation et urbanité dans le Fezzan libyen* (Paris: Karthala, 2003).

[48] The classical English-language reference for the trans-Saharan Sanusiyya network is still Dennis D. Cordell, "Eastern Libya, Wadai and the Sanūsīya: A Ṭarīqa and a Trade Route," *Journal of African History* 18/1 (1977). See also Martel, *La Libye*, 46–82.

[49] In Libyan writings from the period, the Sanusiyya is often only mentioned briefly, if at all: cf. e.g. al-Jarārī, "al-Irth al-tārīkhī," 17–19.

[50] Karine Bennafla, "De la guerre à la coopération : les dangereuses liaisons tchado-libyennes," in *La nouvelle Libye. Sociétés, espaces et géopolitique au lendemain de l'embargo* ed. Olivier Pliez (Paris: Karthala, 2004), 113. On the Sanusi monarchy see also Martel, *La Libye*, 167–90.

[51] The most comprehensive example is Sa'īd 'Abd al-Raḥmān al-Ḥandīrī, *al-'Alāqāt al-lībiyya al-tashādiyya 1842-1975m* (Tripoli: Markaz dirāsat jihād al-lībiyyīn ḍidda al-ghazw al-īṭālī, 1983).

that these historiographic interpretations were also expressions of a specific political context: during the Aouzou Strip dispute and the Libyan military involvement in Chad, that lasted almost twenty years, beginning in 1973, an emphasis on Libyan-Chadian entanglements acquired obvious political implications in a similar way Italian Mediterraneanism had half a century earlier. In fact, Libyan leader Muammar Qaddafi and Chadian president Goukouni Oueddeï in 1981 even agreed on a formal merger between their two states under Libya's *jamāhīriyya* system.[52]

25

But Qaddafi's African policies went well beyond the neighboring state. The formation of the African Union (AU) in his home town Sirt in 1999 was but the most visible instance of Libya's professed pan-Africanism at the time. Despite its original Arab nationalist ideology, the regime in Tripoli had been actively engaged on the continent from its early days as a self-proclaimed "defender of Africa" (*al-mudāfi'a 'an Ifrīqiyā*),[53] supporting independence movements in southern Africa and even intervening directly in several countries (apart from Chad also in Uganda and the Central African Republic). On the African continent, the Libyan regime maybe came closest to the international standing it aspired to. In fact, the Organization of African Unity (OAU) and its successor, the AU, supported Qaddafi in several instances, calling for an end to the United Nations sanctions in the 1990s and trying to mediate during the 2011 uprising and war—whereas the Arab League took the side of the regime's opponents both times. On the occasion of the South African president's visit in 1997 Qaddafi recalled his long-standing support for anti-imperialism on the continent and refuted accusations that he was, in fact, furthering terrorism:

> Mandela is a global leader who is received everywhere with respect, Robert Mugabe is one of Africa's rulers, Sam

---

[52] From the vast literature on Libyan-Chadian relations see in particular John Wright, *Libya, Chad and the Central Sahara* (London: Hurst, 1989); Bennafla, "De la guerre à la coopération."; Judith Scheele, "The Libyan Connection: Settlement, War, and other Entanglements in Northern Chad," *Journal of African History* 57/1 (2016).

[53] Qadhdhāfī, *Thawrat al-fātiḥ*, 95. Of the many biographies of the Libyan leader the best is probably Angelo Del Boca, *Gheddafi. Una sfida dal deserto* (Rome: Laterza, 2010).

> Nujoma is one of Africa's rulers and leaders ... Zenawi
> is now the head of Ethiopia's government, he who was
> called a terrorist, Afewerki who was called a terrorist is
> now president of the Republic of Eritrea, Museveni who
> was called a terrorist, Kabila and his leadership were here
> in the tent and received the support of Libya. Mobutu
> was an agent of Zionism and an agent of imperialism
> then, and they said Libya harbored terrorists ...[54]

Apparently picking up on the historiographical image of Libyans
as bringers of culture and religion, the Libyan Islamic Call Society
(*jam'iyyat al-da'wa al-islāmiyya*) became active in many sub-Saharan
countries. After the oil boom of the 1970s, the Society built mosques
and ran schools or hospitals all over Africa, also in an attempt to
counter the influence of conservative Arab states like Morocco or Saudi
Arabia.[55] The inter-governmental organization Community of Sahel-
Saharan States (CEN-SAD), founded at Tripoli in 1998 to promote
infrastructures and communications across the desert, represented
another Libyan initiative which symbolically tied in with the historic
trans-Saharan networks and demonstrated that the country's vocation
lay beyond the Arab, let alone the Mediterranean, world.[56] As Qaddafi
had summed up his vision at the opening of the African Soccer Cup
in 1982:

> I welcome you on Libyan soil, African brothers [...] Libya
> the defender of Africa, the propagator of the mottos
> 'Africa to the Africans' and 'there is no ally for Africa

[54] Quoted from Sālim Ḥusayn 'Umar al-Barnāwī, "al-'Arab wal-qaḍāyā
al-ifrīqiyya al-mu'āṣira," *Majallat al-buḥūth al-tārīkhiyya* 26/1 (2004), 173.

[55] See Hanspeter Mattes, *Die innere und äußere islamische Mission Libyens.
Historisch-politischer Kontext, innere Struktur, regionale Ausprägung am Beispiel
Afrikas* (Mainz: Grünewald/Kaiser, 1986).

[56] On Qaddafi's African policies see Asteris Huliaras & Konstantinos
Magliveras, "The End of an Affair? Libya and Sub-Saharan Africa," *The
Journal of North African Studies* 16/2 (2011); George Joffé, "Libya's Saharan
Destiny," *The Journal of North African Studies*, 10/3-4 (2005); Yehudit Ronen,
Qaddafi's Libya in World Politics (Boulder: Rienner, 2008), 145–99; Martel,
La Libye, 200–11 and the programmatic speeches in Qadhdhāfī, *Thawrat al-
fātiḥ*.

except itself', Libya that fights imperialism and racism in the defense of Africa ... Libya the guarantor of peace in Chad ... Libya that struggles side by side with the African forces of liberation against the organizations of racist discrimination and against new colonialism [...].[57]

27

Connecting Libya

As Amal Obeidi has shown in an empirical study, in the Libyan population at large identification with the Arab world prevailed and Qaddafi's pan-Africanism remained rather unpopular, even during its supposed heyday in the 1990s.[58] Apart from that, the growing influx of sub-Saharan African migrants also led to conflicts and instances of racism in Libya.[59] Despite all the insistence on the country's African character, Libya remained unmistakably also Arab and Mediterranean. This leads to a third interpretation of Libya's geo-historical situation, namely its function as a bridge between regions and continents. A focus on the history of trans-Saharan trade already hints at transregional networks that go beyond the ties between northern and sub-Saharan Africa:

> In the southern ports of the Mediterranean, such as Algiers, Tunis, or Tripoli, ships from Spanish or Italian cities like Barcelona, Marseilles, Genoa, Pisa, Naples, Bari, or Venice loaded the goods which had come across the Sahara and the Atlas Mountains and shipped them to northern Mediterranean ports where goods had to be unloaded, taxed, and reloaded again, this time onto

---

[57] *Ibid.*, 95.

[58] Amal Obeidi, *Political Culture in Libya* (London: RoutledgeCurzon, 2001), 105–06, 202–09.

[59] See e.g. Chris Dunton, "Black Africans in Libya and Libyan Images of Black Africa," in *The Green and the Black: Qadhafi's Policies in Africa*, ed. René Lemarchand (Bloomington: Indiana University Press, 1988); Ines Kohl, "Nationale Identität, tribale Zugehörigkeit und lokale Konzeptionen im Fezzān, Libyen. Eine Farbenlehre," in *Veränderung und Stabilität. Normen und Werte in islamischen Gesellschaften* ed. Johann Heiss (Vienna: Österreichische Akademie der Wissenschaften, 2005).

horses, donkeys, and oxcarts, and, at least on the Rhone and Rhine, onto riverboats and barges. Goods which went even further north, from Venice via Passau, Linz, Regensburg, or Nuremberg to Prague and Görlitz, eventually reached the southern ports of the Baltic Sea, such as Lübeck, Rostock, or Wismar, where they were reloaded into ships that crossed the Baltic to final destinations in Scandinavia. In contrast, goods that had been unloaded in Timbuktu in the south continued their journey on boats on the Niger and eventually reached destinations on the upper or lower Niger, where they had to be reloaded onto smaller boats or (mostly) donkey and oxen caravans, to be transported into the tropical forests of the Guinea coast, where goods from the north were exchanged for the major product of the south: gold.[60]

In this vein, Nora Lafi has insisted that, up until the 19th century, both "sea and desert were the bases for Tripoli's economic life," while John Wright has called the Libyan capital an "entrepot serving three continents."[61]

Libyan historians, too, have not just presented the African dimension of their country's history, but also linked this back to its Arab and Mediterranean roots and even to Europe. Authors repeatedly claimed that different locations, for instance the town of Ghadames or the region of Fezzan, have been "gateways to the Sahara" and Ḥabīb al-Ḥasnāwī even defined Libya as a whole as "Europe's gateway to Africa."[62] But apart from constituting "the link between the center of

---

[60] Roman Loimeier, *Muslim Societies in Africa: A Historical Anthropology* (Bloomington: Indiana University Press, 2013), 58.

[61] Nora Lafi, *Une ville du Maghreb entre ancien régime et réformes ottomanes. Genèse des institutions municipales à Tripoli de Barbarie (1795-1911)* (Paris: L'Harmattan, 2002), 53; Wright, *The Emergence of Libya*, 130.

[62] E.g. Sharaf al-Din, "Tijārat Ṭarābulus," 150; Imḥammad Saʿīd al-Ṭawīl, "al-Ṣirāʿ al-duwalī ʿalā madīnat Ghadāmis khilāla al-niṣf al-thānī min al-qarn al-tāsiʿ ʿashar wa-inʿikāsātuhu ʿalā tijāratihā," in *Aʿmāl al-nadwa al-ʿilmiyya al-tārīkhiyya ḥawla tārīkh Ghadāmis min khilāli kitābāt al-raḥḥāla wal-muʾarrikhīn*, ed. Nūr al-Dīn Muṣṭafa al-Thinnī (Tripoli: Markaz jihād al-lībiyyīn lil-dirāsāt al-tārīkhiyya, 2003), 202; Ḥabīb Wadaʿ al-Ḥasnāwī, "Lībiyā fī faḍāʾay al-Baḥr al-mutawassiṭ wa-Ifrīqiyā wa-ʿalāqatuhā maʿa Firansā," *Majal-*

Africa and the outside world", it was equally "the bridge that connects East and West of the Arab homeland."[63] The Iraqi art historian Ṣabā Qays al-Yāsirī in a contribution to Libya's major historical journal argued that the country had functioned as a link between geographical regions from Antiquity to the present. Although she mentioned the ancient Phoenicians as well as medieval Muslim scholars, the main argument was apparently, once again, Libya's role as a commercial hub:

29

> Tripoli is characterized by its strategic maritime position which made it over the centuries, faster than the other commercial centers, into a link between the countries of southern Europe and the Arab Maghreb. The trading caravans across the Sahara brought all sorts of goods that were known at the time from the sub-Saharan regions, and also from the Arab Mashreq, to Tripoli. Tripoli had always been a city of extensive commerce, its only competitor being Alexandria, and ships from Malta, Venice, and Sicily used to dock in its port to engage perpetually in trade. Apart from that, it is known that Libya was, and still is, the region that connects East and West of the Islamic world.[64]

Emerging at the center of multiple connections, Libya's history, thus understood, presented various overlapping dimensions that historians have defined as Mediterranean, Arab, African, Maghribi, Ottoman, and Southern.[65]

---

lat al-buḥūth al-tārīkhiyya 30/1 (2008), 19.

[63] Muḥammad ʿAli Abū Shārib, "Tijārat al-qawāfil wa-ʿalāqatuhā bi-wāḥat Awjila," in *Awjila bayna al-māḍī wal-ḥāḍir (1550-1951m): Aʿmāl al-nad-wa al-ʿilmiyya al-sābiʿa allatī ʿuqidat bi-madīnat Awjila (17-20/9/2000)* ed. Muhammad Bashir Suwaysi (Tripoli: Markaz jihād al-lībiyyīn lil-dirāsāt al-tārīkhiyya, 2007), 131.

[64] Ṣabā Qays al-Yāsirī, "Dawr wa-ahammiyyat Lībiyā ka-ḥalqat waṣl bayna al-sharq wal-gharb fī al-tārīkh," *Majallat al-buḥūth al-tārīkhiyya* 30/1 (2008), 99.

[65] See Ḥasnāwī, "Lībiyā fī faḍāʾay al-Baḥr al-mutawassiṭ wa-Ifrīqiyā."; Jāsim Muḥammad Shaṭb al-ʿUbaydi, "al-Tijāra al-ṣaḥrāwiyya wal-masʾala al-sharqiyya fī al-qarn al-tāsiʿ ʿashar wa-maṭlaʿa al-qarn al-ʿishrīn," *Majallat al-buḥūth al-tārīkhiyya* 30/1 (2008). On the overlapping and competing identifications see also Martel, *La Libye*, 15-42.

Again, it might not be a coincidence that the idea of Libya as a connecting link (*ḥalqat waṣl*) has become particularly prominent since about the year 2000.[66] In fact, the last phase of the Qaddafi regime from 1998 to 2010 was characterized by a rapprochement with the West in foreign policy and a liberalization of the economy. Apart from that, Libya had become an important region of transit but also a destination for migrants from sub-Saharan Africa from the 1990s onward.[67] Both trade deals—regarding oil, in particular—and agreements on migration control with the European Union as a whole and single countries north of the Mediterranean actually contributed a lot to the diffusion of the notion of Libya as a bridge between regions and continents. With the uncertainty about the country's future following instability and civil war since 2011, the question of Libya's geopolitical orientation— Mediterranean, African, or connecting—remains as significant and as open as ever.

---

[66] But see also already Africanus, "Geopolitica di Gheddafi."

[67] See e.g. Ronen, *Qaddafi's Libya*, 54–75; Sara Hamood, "EU-Libya Coop-eration on Migration: A Raw Deal for Refugees and Migrants?" *Journal of Refugee Studies* 21/1 (2008); Derek Lutterbeck, "Migrants, Weapons and Oil: Europe and Libya after the Sanctions," *The Journal of North African Studies* 14/2 (2009); Amir M. Kamel, "Trade and Peace: The EU and Qaddafi's Final Decade," *International Affairs* 92/3 (2016).

Bibliography

Abulafia, David. "Mediterraneans." In *Rethinking the Mediterranean*, ed. W. V. Harris, 64–93. Oxford: Oxford University Press, 2005.

Abū Shārib, Muḥammad 'Alī. "Tijārat al-qawāfil wa-'alāqatuhā bi-wāḥat Awjila." In *Awjila bayna al-māḍī wal-ḥāḍir (1550-1951m): A'māl al-nadwa al-'ilmiyya al-sābi'a allatī 'uqidat bi-madīnat Awjila (17-20/9/2000)*, ed. M. B. Suwaysi, 131–144. Tripoli: Markaz jihād al-lībiyyīn lil-dirāsāt al-tārīkhiyya, 2007.

Africanus, "Geopolitica di Gheddafi: realismo travestito da stravaganza." *Limes* 2 (1994), 107–117.

Ahmida, Ali Abdullatif, ed. *Bridges across the Sahara: Social, Economic and Cultural Impact of the Trans-Sahara Trade during the 19th and 20th Centuries*. Newcastle: Cambridge Scholars, 2011.

Altekamp, Stefan. *Rückkehr nach Afrika. Italienische Kolonialarchäologie in Libyen 1911-1943*. Cologne: Böhlau, 2000.

Aurigemma, Salvatore. "Il Castello di Tripoli di Barberia." In *La rinascita della Tripolitania. Memorie e studi sui quattro anni di governo del Conte Giuseppe Volpi di Misurata*, ed. A. Piccioli, 535–563. Milan: Arnoldo Mondadori, 1926.

Austen, Ralph A. *Trans-Saharan Africa in World History*. New York: Oxford University Press, 2010.

al-Barnāwī, Sālim Ḥusayn. "al-'Arab wal-qaḍāyā al-ifrīqiyya al-mu'āṣira." *Majallat al-buḥūth al-tārīkhiyya* 26/1 (2004): 155–214.

Bennafla, Karine. "De la guerre à la coopération : les dangereuses liaisons tchado-libyennes." In *La nouvelle Libye. Sociétés, espaces et géopolitique au lendemain de l'embargo*, ed. O. Pliez, 111–137. Paris: Karthala, 2004.

Birley, Anthony R. *The African Emperor: Septimius Severus*. London: Batsford, 1988.

Braudel, Fernand. *The Mediterranean and the Mediterranean World in the Age of Philip II*, trans. S. Reynolds. New York: Harper & Row, 1972.

Cordell, Dennis D. "Eastern Libya, Wadai and the Sanūsīya: A Ṭarīqa and a Trade Route." *Journal of African History* 18/1 (1977): 21–36.

Cresti, Federico. *Non desiderare la terra d'altri. La colonizzazione italiana in Libia*. Rome: Carocci, 2011.

D'Annunzio, Gabriele. *Laudi del cielo del mare della terra e degli eroi*. Milan: Treves, 1912.

Del Boca, Angelo. *Gheddafi. Una sfida dal deserto*. Rome: Laterza, 2010.

Del Boca, Angelo. "L'Impero." In *I luoghi della memoria. Simboli e miti dell'Italia unita*, ed. M. Isnenghi. Rome: Laterza, 1996.

Dumasy, François. "L'autre et soi même. Les usages du passé médiéval dans la Libye coloniale au miroir de la construction nationale italienne." In *Maghreb-Italie. Des passeurs médiévaux à l'orientalisme moderne (XIIIᵉ - milieu XXᵉ siècle)*, ed. B. Grévin, 373–395. Rome: École française de Rome, 2010.

Dunton, Chris. "Black Africans in Libya and Libyan Images of Black Africa." In *The Green and the Black: Qadhafi's Policies in Africa*, ed. R. Lemarchand, 150–166. Bloomington: Indiana University Press, 1988.

al-Faytūrī, Aḥmad. "al-Jāliyāt al-'arabiyya al-mubakkira fī bilād al-Sūdān: Dirāsa awwaliyya wa-ba'ḍ al-mulāḥaẓāt." *Majallat al-buḥūth al-tārīkhiyya* 3/2 (1981), 245–252.

Fuller, Mia. "Preservation and Self-Absorption: Italian Colonisation and the Walled City of Tripoli, Libya." *The Journal of North African Studies* 5/4 (2000), 121–154.

Fuller, Mia. *Moderns Abroad: Architecture, Cities and Italian Imperialism.* Abingdon: Routledge, 2010.

Gentile, Emilio. "6 maggio 1936. L'Impero torna a Roma." In *I giorni di Roma. Nove grandi storici raccontano nove giornate cruciali per la storia di Roma e del mondo*, ed. A. Carandini et al., 239–270. Rome: Laterza, 2007.

Haarmann, Ulrich. "The Dead Ostrich: Life and Trade in Ghadames (Libya) in the Nineteenth Century." *Die Welt des Islams* 38/1 (1998), 9–94.

Hamood, Sara. "EU-Libya Cooperation on Migration: A Raw Deal for Refugees and Migrants?" *Journal of Refugee Studies* 21/1 (2008), 19–42.

al-Ḥandīrī, Sa'īd 'A. *al-'Alāqāt al-lībiyya al-tašādiyya 1842-1975m.* Tripoli: Markaz dirāsat jihād al-lībiyyīn ḍidda al-ghazw al-īṭālī, 1983.

al-Ḥasnāwī, Ḥabīb Wadā'a. "Lībiyā fī faḍā'ay al-Baḥr al-mutawassiṭ wa-Ifrīqiyā wa-'alāqatuhā ma'a Firansā." *Majallat al-buḥūth al-tārīkhiyya* 30/1 (2008), 17–55.

von Henneberg, Krystyna. "Tripoli: Piazza Castello and the Making of a Fascist Colonial Capital." In *Streets: Critical Perspectives on Public Space*, eds. Z. Çelik, D. Favro & R. Ingersoll, 136–150. Berkeley: University of California Press, 1996.

Huliaras, Asteris & Magliveras, Konstantinos. "The End of an Affair? Libya and Sub-Saharan Africa." *The Journal of North African Studies* 16/2 (2011), 167–181.

al-Ḥurayr, 'Abd al-Mawlā Ṣāliḥ. "al-Islām wa-atharuhu 'alā al-taṭawwurāt al-siyāsiyya wal-fikriyya wal-iqtiṣādiyya fī Ifrīqiyā janūb al-Ṣaḥrā'." *Majallat al-buḥūth al-tārīkhiyya* 11/2 (1989), 97–136.

al-Ḥurayr, Idrīs Ṣāliḥ. "al-'Alāqāt al-iqtiṣādiyya wal-thaqāfiyya bayna al-dawla al-rustamiyya wa-buldān janūb al-Ṣaḥrā' al-kubrā wa-atharuhā fī nashar al-islām hunāk." *Majallat al-buḥūth al-tārīkhiyya* 5/1 (1983), 75–87.

Ḥusayn, Aḥmad Ilyās. "Ṭuruq al-tijāra fī al-juz' al-sharqī min al-Ṣaḥrā' al-kubrā." In *al-Ṣaḥrā' al-kubrā: Kitāb tidhkārī yataḍamman dirāsāt mutarjama wa-aṣliyya ṣadara bi-munāsabat in'iqād al-nadwa al-'ilmiyya al-'ālamiyya lil-tijāra 'abra al-Ṣaḥrā', Ṭarābulus min 2-4 uktūbar 1979*, ed. 'I. Ghanim, 111–115. Tripoli: Markaz buḥūth wa-dirāsāt al-jihād al-lībī, 1979.

al-Jarārī, Muḥammad al-Ṭāhir. "al-Irth al-tārīkhī lil-ṣilāt al-'arabiyya al-ifrīqiyya - Lībiyā numūdhajan."*Majallat al-buḥūth al-tārīkhiyya* 26/1 (2004), 11–28.

Jerary, Mohammed Taher. "Septimius Severus: The Roman Emperor, 193-211 AD."*Africa* 63/2 (2008), 173–185.

Joffé, George. "Libya's Saharan Destiny." *The Journal of North African Studies* 10/3-4 (2005), 605–617.

Kamel, Amir Mohammed. "Trade and Peace: The EU and Qaddafi's Final Decade." *International Affairs* 92/3 (2016), 683–702.

Kohl, Ines. "Nationale Identität, tribale Zugehörigkeit und lokale Konzeptionen im Fezzān, Libyen. Eine Farbenlehre." In *Veränderung und Stabilität. Normen und Werte in islamischen Gesellschaften*, ed. J. Heiss, 137–168. Vienna: Österreichische Akademie der Wissenschaften, 2005.

Krais, Jakob. *Geschichte als Widerstand. Geschichtsschreibung und* nation-building *in Qaḏḏāfīs Libyen*. Würzburg: Ergon, 2016.

Lafi, Nora. *Une ville du Maghreb entre ancien régime et réformes ottomanes. Genèse des institutions municipales à Tripoli de Barbarie (1795-1911)*. Paris: L'Harmattan, 2002.

La Mantia, Giuseppe. "La Sicilia ed il suo dominio nell'Africa settentrionale dal secolo XI al XVI." *Archivio storico siciliano* 44 (1922), 154–265.

Loimeier, Roman. *Muslim Societies in Africa: A Historical Anthropology*. Bloomington: Indiana University Press, 2013.

Lopez, Roberto S. *Storia delle colonie genovesi nel Mediterraneo*. Genoa: Marietti, 1997.

33

Lutterbeck, Derek. "Migrants, Weapons and Oil: Europe and Libya after the Sanctions." *The Journal of North African Studies* 14/2 (2009), 169–184.

34

Manfroni, Camillo. *I colonizzatori italiani durante il Medio Evo e il Rinascimento*, vol. I: *Dal secolo XI al XIII*; vol. II: *Dal secolo XIV al XVI - Con un'appendice sulle vicende delle colonie veneziane fino al secolo XVIII*. Rome: Libreria dello Stato, 1934.

Manfroni, Camillo. *L'Italia nelle vicende marinare della Tripolitania*. Intra: Airoldi, 1935.

Manfroni, Camillo. *Storia della marina italiana*, vol. I: *Dalle invasioni barbariche al trattato di Ninfeo (anni di C. 400-1261)*; vol. III: *Dalla caduta di Costantinopoli alla battaglia di Lepanto*. Milan: Periodici Scientifici, 1970.

Martel, André. *La Libye 1835-1990. Essai de géopolitique historique*. Paris: PUF, 1991.

Mattes, Hanspeter. *Die innere und äußere islamische Mission Libyens. Historisch-politischer Kontext, innere Struktur, regionale Ausprägung am Beispiel Afrikas*. Mainz: Grünewald/Kaiser, 1986.

Mattingly, David J. *Imperialism, Power, and Identity: Experiencing the Roman Empire*. Princeton: Princeton University Press, 2011.

McDougall, James. "Frontiers, Borderlands, and Saharan/World History." In *Saharan Frontiers: Space and Mobility in Northwest Africa*, ed. J. McDougall & J. Scheele, 73–91. Bloomington: Indiana University Press, 2012.

McLaren, Brian L. *Architecture and Tourism in Italian Colonial Libya: An Ambivalent Modernism*. Seattle: University of Washington Press, 2006.

Merighi, Antonio. *La Tripolitania antica. Dalle origini alla invasione degli arabi*. Verbania: Airoldi, 1940.

Munzi, Massimiliano. *L'epica del ritorno. Archeologia e politica nella Tripolitania italiana*. Rome: L'Erma di Bretschneider, 2001.

Obeidi, Amal. *Political Culture in Libya*. London: RoutledgeCurzon, 2001.

Pliez, Olivier. *Villes du Sahara. Urbanisation et urbanité dans le Fezzan libyen*. Paris: Karthala, 2003.

al-Qadhdhāfī, Mu'ammar. *Thawrat al-fātiḥ wa-Ifrīqiyā*. Tripoli: al-Markaz al-'ālamī li-dirāsāt wa-abḥāth al-Kitāb al-akhḍar, 1985.

Rava, Carlo Emilio. "Di un'architettura coloniale moderna - Parte prima." *Domus* 4/5 (1931), 39–43.

Romanelli, Pietro. *Vestigia del passato (monumenti e scavi)*. Rome: Ministero delle Colonie, Ufficio studi e propaganda, 1930.

Romano, Sergio. *Giuseppe Volpi. Industria e finanza tra Giolitti e Mussolini.* Milan: Bompiani, 1979.

Ronen, Yehudit. *Qaddafi's Libya in World Politics.* Boulder: Rienner, 2008.

Rossi, Ettore. *Il dominio degli Spagnoli e dei Cavalieri di Malta a Tripoli (1510-1551). Con appendice di documenti dell'archivio dell'Ordine a Malta.* Intra: Airoldi, 1937.

Scheele, Judith. "The Libyan Connection: Settlement, War, and other Entanglements in Northern Chad." *Journal of African History* 57/1 (2016), 115–134.

Segrè, Claudio G. *Italo Balbo: A Fascist Life.* Berkeley: University of California Press, 1990.

Sharaf al-Dīn, Limyā'. "Tijārat Ṭarābulus ma'a bilād mā warā'a al-Ṣaḥrā' fī al-'aṣr al-wasīṭ." *Majallat al-buḥūth al-tārīkhiyya* 23/2 (2001), 141–159.

Shaṭb al-'Ubaydi, Jāsim Muḥammad. "al-Tijāra al-ṣaḥrāwiyya walmas'ala al-sharqiyya fī al-qarn al-tāsi' 'ashar wa-maṭla'a al-qarn al-'ishrīn." *Majallat al-buḥūth al-tārīkhiyya* 30/1 (2008), 117–155.

Silva, Pietro. *Il Mediterraneo. Dall'unità di Roma all'Impero italiano.* Milan: Istituto per gli studi di politica internazionale, 1937.

Tamburini, Olga. "'La via romana sepolta dal mare': mito del *Mare nostrum* e ricerca di un'identità nazionale." In *Mare nostrum. Percezione ottomana e mito mediterraneo in Italia all'alba del '900,* ed. S. Trinchese, 41–95. Milan: Guerini, 2005.

al-Ṭawīl, Imḥammad Sa'īd. "al-Ṣirā' al-duwalī 'alā madīnat Ghadāmis khilāla al-niṣf al-thānī min al-qarn al-tāsi' 'ashar wa-in'ikāsātuhu 'alā tijāratihā." In *A'māl al-nadwa al-'ilmiyya al-tārīkhiyya ḥawla tārīkh Ghadāmis min khilāli kitābāt al-raḥḥāla wal-mu'arrikhīn,* ed. N. M. al-Thinnī, 195–215. Tripoli: Markaz jihād al-lībiyyīn lil-dirāsāt al-tārīkhiyya, 2003.

Valérian, Dominiques. "Lectures italiennes de l'expansion latine dans le Maghreb médiéval (première moitié du XXe siècle)." In *Maghreb-Italie. Des passeurs médiévaux à l'orientalisme moderne (XIIIe - milieu XXe siècle),* ed. B. Grévin, 343–356. Rome: École française de Rome, 2010.

Vinassa de Regny, Paolo. *Libya Italica. Terreni ed acque, vita e colture della nuova colonia.* Milan: Hoepli, 1913.

Volpe, Gioacchino. *Italia moderna,* vol. I: *1815-1898.* Florence: Sansoni, 1958.

Volpi di Misurata, Giuseppe. *La Repubblica di Venezia e i suoi*

35

ambasciatori. Lezione tenuta alla R.Università Italiana di Perugia per Stranieri il 21 Settembre 1927. Milan: Arnoldo Mondadori, 1928.

Wright, John. *The Emergence of Libya: Selected Historical Essays.* London: Silphium Press/The Society for Libyan Studies, 2008.

Wright, John. *Libya, Chad and the Central Sahara.* London: Hurst, 1989.

al-Yāsirī, Ṣabā Qays. "Dawr wa-ahammiyyat Lībiyā ka-ḥalqat waṣl bayna al-sharq wal-gharb fī al-tārīkh." *Majallat al-buḥūth al-tārīkhiyya* 30/1 (2008), 95–115.

36

CHRISTOPHE PEREIRA

37

The Construction of Virility and Performance of Masculinities in the Language Practices of Young Men in Tripoli *

Abstract: This article analyzes the socio/linguistic construction of gender in Arabic in Tripoli, showing how young Libyan men make use of virile and masculine speech practices as part of their performance of gender. Analyzing the interactions of a group of young men through participant observation and a resulting corpus of spontaneous recordings of speech, this article shows how, in their self-expression, certain young Libyan men perform their speech practices towards hegemonic, gendered goals, exalting virilizing values and foregrounding heterosexism by means of transgressive language practices. These language practices express domination, heterosexism, and homosociality, permitting them to distinguish themselves from women and others discursively and interactively constructed as inferiors, in order to validate their existence as dominant males.

Keywords: *Tripoli, Libyan Arabic, gender, masculinities, heterosexism, homosociality*

IF GENDER STUDIES HAS TURNED above all to history, sociology, and philosophy, linguistics has also renewed its own approaches in order to explore the ways in which gender is performed via situated interactions.[1] This article situates itself among these perspectives in

---

* The core of this article corresponds to the section concerning Libya in a co-authored article on the construction of masculinities in Morocco and Libya, to which I have added further examples and a more extensive introduction. The original text was translated from French for this publication by Adam Benkato, whom I warmly thank. For that original piece, see Moïse, Claudine, Christophe Pereira, Ángeles Vicente, and Karima Ziamari, "La construction socio-langagière du genre: jeunes hommes libyens, jeunes femmes marocaines et rapport à la masculinité," in *Sociolinguistique des pratiques langagières de jeunes*, ed. C. Trimaille, C. Pereira, K. Ziamari, and M. Gasquet-Cyrus (Grenoble: UGA Éditions, 2020), 81–115.

38

order to examine the co-construction of the category "masculine" via situated language practices. It is based on the consideration of gender as a construction that is both social and relational as well as linguistic and situated, one that expressed relations of domination between men and women which are determined economically, ethnically, and socially. On the basis of interactions in Libyan Arabic, this article will analyze how certain young Libyan men perform their speech towards gendered, hegemonic aims in their self-expression.

From a methodological point of view, it is important to note my relationship to my interlocutors and the conditions in which I was able to collect the material which allowed me to write this article. In fact, I did not initially carry out fieldwork with the specific goal of collecting information pertaining to the performance of masculinities, but rather originally with the goal of gathering data which would permit me to write a grammatical description of the Arabic variety of Tripoli.[2] The particularity of my approach here results from the position which I adopted: that of a researcher who immerses and implicates themself in their field of inquiry in order to accumulate empirical data which ultimately leads to a description of linguistic and social realities. In other words, I was a participant-observer.

This position, or posture, so to speak—which permitted me to become familiar with the Tripolitanian milieu and to gather the firsthand data which would later lead to my initial published works— could not have been maintained without the complicity, that is, both the consent and supporting actions, of local actors. During my first trip to Tripoli, I had the chance to get to know young men of the same age as myself, who would become my close friends and open unique perspectives up to me. Thanks to these friends, I was able to travel regularly to and around Tripoli and engage intimately with Libyan society while being immersed within their social group and sharing their lifestyles, all while observing their linguistic practices. I thus obtained from these young interlocutors, in a somewhat natural way, a

---

[1] See for example Deborah Cameron, "Gender, Language and Discourse: A Review Essay," *Signs* 23 (1998), 945–973.

[2] Christophe Pereira, *Le parler arabe de Tripoli (Libye)* (Zaragoza: IEIOP, 2010).

corpus which could reflect contemporary linguistic practices in Tripoli. This type of fieldwork praxis, consisting of sharing the lifestyle of one's interlocutors in order to absorb their codes and of participating in their group activities in order to learn their social practices, allowed me to become one of their own. Because of living in an immersive situation with my interlocutors, according to the rhythms of their lives, I was able to become capable with spoken Arabic, gaining familiarity with my interlocutors' language at the same time that I gained familiarity with their city and their culture. These young men accorded me their confidence, appreciated my interest in their mother tongue, and allowed me to record even their most intimate conversations.

Born towards the end of the 1970s, these interlocutors represent in some ways the ideal generation for the examination of the formation and development of the Arabic variety of Tripoli, reflecting the impact of massive urbanization as well as the effects of political measures on language use in society. But they are also representative of young Libyan men on the path to adulthood, in a period of transition after the end of their studies and prior to marriage, and who are frustrated and in search of diversions in a social and urban context in which they often felt bored. It is precisely at this stage of their lives when I was present and could experience firsthand how they promoted "virilizing" values among themselves while foregrounding heterosexism through transgressive language practices. It is on the basis of these real-life conversations between young people, captured in a natural way and in an intimate setting, that I was able to comprehend this familiar and coarse vocabulary, one including sexually connotative expressions. It was thus my participant observation which allowed me to obtain data regarding sexuality, the performance of masculinities, and the expression of domination which I describe in this article. The goal of writing such a paper is thus to describe the language practices of young Tripolitanian men, at a particular moment in their lives, and indeed also in the life of the Tripoli dialect, and at a precise moment in their history—to describe linguistic facts in connection with social realities. It is this which led me to observe and describe the construction of masculinities: how are these masculinities performed? How are they reflected in interactions? And to what ends?

In the first part of this article, I will briefly contextualize the corpus along with some elements which aid in the comprehension of the social context in which these young men were developing. Then in the second part, I will attempt to describe precisely how these young men perform masculinities, via situated language practices, while reflecting their heterosexism: via a transgressive style and gendered insults (by way of terms of address or subjugation of others), claiming their heterosexuality through gendered self-presentation, in order to thus distinguish themselves from others discursively and interactionally constructed as inferior, and ultimately prove their existence as heterosexual, dominant males.

Contextualizing the Corpus

Although there exist stereotypes regarding masculinity, such as gender differences, heterosexism, domination, and homosociality,[3] there is no universal masculine model valid for all times and all places. Since there is no such thing as a universal model of masculinity and since masculinity varies historically, socially, and between generations, it is more accurate to speak of masculinities in the plural.[4] These cannot be envisaged without taking into account the social structures, cultural values, and systems of beliefs and practices in which they are constructed. Consequently, even if they are performed in interactions, the observation of masculinities through the language practices of young men cannot ignore their socio-cultural context.

The Interlocutors

The recordings on which this study is based were gathered in Tripoli between 2000 and 2011. The interlocutors were all born towards the end of the 1970s, were inhabitants of the Libyan capital, were Muslim by upbringing as well as practice, and at the time of fieldwork were all unmarried and still living with their parents. They had just finished their studies (all studied engineering) and possessed doubts about their future prospects: they would soon be finding themselves needing to

---

[3] See Scott Kiesling, "Men, Masculinities and Language," *Blackwell Linguistics and Language Compass* 1/6 (2007), 657.

[4] See Raewyn Connell, *Masculinities* (Berkeley: University of California Press, 2005).

face the responsibilities of obtaining work and getting married—or to put it another way, needing to acquire the attributes of an adult male. Moreover, their comportment and their discourse also evoked their heterosexuality. This period in their lives corresponds to a moment on the path towards adulthood called "emerging adulthood" by Arnett.[5] It is an ideal phase in which to examine the correlation between these young men's linguistic habits and the elaboration of their masculinities as well as the expression of their virility.

41

Gathering the Data

During my fieldwork in Tripoli, I was able to cultivate a relationship of friendship and trust with this group of young men, where they allowed me to record them without limit while having access to their most intimate conversations, particularly those which dealt with taboo subjects, especially sexuality. These recordings were always made in private, away from those who were not part of the peer group. Outside of this group, discretion was the rule, owing especially to fear of being blamed for indiscretion by those external to it. On this subject, they would say:

l-lībi yəḥšəm m-əl-lībi

"The Libyan (man) shows shame in front of the
Libyan (man)"

Because of this, it was frequently in the car during casual drives that my interlocutors would feel comfortable enough to speak spontaneously about the things most intimate to them—the car was one of the rare spaces of escape and of freedom for young Libyan men, especially growing up in a closed society. Libya between 2000 and 2011 (again, the period of my fieldwork there) was a relatively conservative Muslim country, but also one in which severe social and political oppression governed the use of language and linguistic practice. The present essay deals therefore with social practices situated in a certain time and

---

[5] Jeffrey Arnett, "Emerging Adulthood. A Theory of Development From the Late Teens Through the Twenties," *American Psychologist* 55/5 (2000), 469–480.

place, and which recent and current upheavals may be in the process of reconfiguring.

From *ksād* and frustration...

In Libya at the time, activities through which one could relieve physical and emotional tension were rare, not to speak of the fact that alcohol was (and still is) officially prohibited and where the only way for young single men to have adventures was recourse to certain semi-legal sexual services.[6] Numerous terms and expressions used in everyday language recall this context. The term *ksād* "boredom, stagnation, depression," as well as the participle from the same root *mkəssəd* "bored, stagnant, depressing," terms with a great deal of semantic charge, designate this emptiness, this lassitude. In it, the everyday is monotonous, as one interlocutor describes in a humorous tone:

kull yōm nafs-əl-bərnāməž...

"Every day the same program..."

Not to speak of Friday, the lone day off of the week, of which the same interlocutor says:

ḥne ʕand-na yōm-əž-žumʕa ksād ḥālba,
tgūl tlāt ayyām lāṣgāt fi baʕḍ

"For us Friday is extremely boring; you'd say
it's like three days stuck to each other..."

Faced with the fatalism of events, these young men were nevertheless capable of humor and self-mockery. In a situation of constant submission (to one's family and to the weight of tradition), of fear of political repression (the regime depriving them of basic freedoms), but also of social injustice (they live in a major exporter of oil and gas but

---

[6] Christophe Pereira, "Les mots de la sexualité dans l'arabe de Tripoli (Libye): désémantisation, grammaticalisation et évolution linguistique," in *L'Année du Maghreb. Numéro VI. Dossier: Sexualités au Maghreb: Essais d'ethnographies contemporaines*, ed. V. Beaumont, C. Cauvin Verner & F. Pouillon (Paris: CNRS Editions, 2010), 117–140.

must still ask why that the benefits of that massive revenue are not visible), a profound sentiment of rage is evident. Anxious about their destiny, they would say:

ə*l-qadər mnayyək ya ʕənn-dīn-kum!*

"Fate is fucked up, curse your religion!"

They were nostalgic for the period in which they were students, during which their responsibilities and obligations were deferred:

R)   (laughs) *hādi l-xədma əlli təbbi dīn-umm-ha*

"(laughs) This is the work which needs its mother's religion."

A)   *wuḷḷāhi..*

"Really."

N)   *mā-nəbbī-hā-š āne wuḷḷāhi mā-nəbbī-ha* (laughs)

"I don't want it, I don't. Seriously, I do not want it (laughs)."

A)   *wuḷḷāhi l-gaḥba kāna irəddū-na*

"I swear, bitch, if we could just get taken back."

R)   *b-əs-sēf wuḷḷāhi b-əs-sēf. bāh, šən bə-tdīr?*

"By force, seriously, by force. Alright, what would you do?"

A)   *kāna irəddū-na ṭaḷaba?*

"If we could just get taken back (to when we were students)?"

N)   *kāna kāna ya gaḥbət lə-ghāb kāna…*

"If only, if only, oh whore of whores, if only…"

These young men's conversations were frequently punctuated by mocking laughs. They accuse their jobs of being responsible for their ills (*hādi l-xədma əlli təbbi dīn-umm-ha*) all while knowing they would have no alternative, hence the use of the adverbial expression *b-əs-sēf* "by force, inevitably." Despite their refusal to accept this new situation (*mā-nəbbī-hā-š āne wuḷḷāhi mā-nəbbī-ha*) and their regret at being unable to go back in time to when they were students (*wuḷḷāhi l-gaḥba kāna iṛəddū-na [...] kāna iṛəddū-na ṭaḷaba*) they were quickly captured by their fate: *b-əs-sēf wuḷḷāhi b-əs-sēf. bāh, šən bə-tdīr?* The final sentence of the text, the saying *kāna kāna ya gaḥbət lə-ġḥāb kāna* (a vulgar equivalent to "if wishes were horses, beggars would ride"), brings an end to their pipe dream. It is notably humor which allows the diffusing of personal tensions: a loophole intensified by recourse to a crude but playful language specific to young men.

...to attempts at escape

Faced with malaise, these young men desired change in their lives, effervescence and stimulating perspectives; a recurrent theme in their conversations was hence the possibility of traveling.

A)   *āne tawwa nəbbi ndīr bərnāməž, nəbbi ndəss gəṛšēn, nəmši lə-fṛansa...*

"Me, right now I want to make a plan, I want to save some money and go to France..."

R)   *šən bə-tdīr?*

"What do you intend to do?"

A)   *nəmši l-fṛansa kāna xdēt əl-kurs āhuwa w əl-kurs əž-žāy fṛansāwi, nəbbi nəmši l-fṛansa...*

"I'll go to France, if I took this course and the next course, French, I want to go to France..."

R)   *təmši ʕale ḥsāb-ak?*

"You'll go with your own money?"

A)   *nəmši nnīk sbūʕēn tlāta ġādi nḥaṛṛək bī-hum lsān-i f-əl-fṛansāwi lākən baʕd-ma nnīk daʕəm...fa mumkən nəmši nnīk mtāʕ tlāt āsābīʕ hekke ʕand hūwa šwēya ʕand hūwa šwēya ʕand hūwa šwēya bārīs hekke nšūf bārīs lākən nəbbi gəṛšēn ndəss-hum fhəmt-ni?*

"I'll go, fuck around for two or three weeks over
there, get my tongue moving in French, but after
(having got) some fucking (financial) support...So
maybe I'll go fuck around for around three weeks,
something like that, a little here, a little there,
a little here, Paris is like that, I'll see Paris but I
want to save money, you know what I mean?"

R) *təbbi l-ha ēh hādi təbbi gəṛšēn ēh təbbi mabləġ u
    bārīs ġālya ḷ-az̧-z̧oḅḅ !*

    "It needs it, yea, this needs some money, yea,
    it needs a (large) amount and Paris is damn
    expensive!"

Alleging some excuse (*nəmši nnīk sbūʕēn tlāta ġādi nḥaṛṛək bī-hum
lsān-i f-əl-fṛanṣāwi*) this short-term plan was entirely feasible before the
obligations of adult life, on condition of having built up some savings,
such as is largely recalled in the preceding dialog: *nəbbi ndəss gəṛšēn;
lākən nəbbi gəṛšēn ndəss-hum; ēh hādi təbbi gəṛšēn ēh təbbi mabləġ u
bārīs ġālya ḷ-az̧-z̧oḅḅ*, where *gəṛšēn* literally means "two piasters" and
mabləġ means "sum of money". Beyond linguistic concerns, one can
see in these last examples that getaway trip in a foreign country would
have given them access to activities they would not normally have in
Libya, notably to quench their thirst and staunch their hunger, so to
speak. As mentioned before, Libya was (and still is) a country where
alcohol was officially prohibited and where the only way for young
single men to have liaisons was recourse to certain semi-legal sexual
services.[7] While they waited to have saved enough money to travel,
prostitution appears as a more affordable and local way to appease the
unsatisfied spirits of these young men who would have liked a more
available sexuality:

N) *fi fṛanṣa ġādi ya matyəs ā-hu ngūl l-ək ʕlāš ḍʕif
    anta...antu fi fṛanṣa tnīku dīma (laughs) ḥne
    n-nēk nəšbḥu fī-h maṛṛa fi sana*

    "Over there in France, you fags [=goats], here
    I'll tell you why you're skinny. You in France, you

---

[7] See again Pereira, "Les mots de la sexualité."

fuck all the time (laughs), we, we get a fuck once a year..."

46   R)   *ḥne ʕādi əl-lībīyīn dīma nēk...*

"We Libyans (would be) fine to fuck all the time..."

A)   *ṭabʕan mā-ʕand-hum-š muškila...*

"Of course, they wouldn't have a problem..."

N)   *ḥne l-lībīyīn māda bī-na dīma nēk māda bī-na...*

"We Libyans, we would like to fuck all the time, we'd like that..."

As their main way of escaping the grip of reality, these young men have, of course, their fantasies and their imagination—but it is in reality that they must seek escape in order to confront their daily life: moments of relaxation and diversion among friends. Spirits calm among members of a peer group, in a male social space. This is an important space of socialization and of rare freedoms and it is valued for this very reason. It is far enough away from the observation of their families, from peers outside of their immediate group, and from the secret services, that these young men could unwind, disengage, and find relief. There, through their linguistic practices in particular, they affirm their virility and perform their masculinities.[8]

Virility, masculinities, and linguistic practices

In a society of asymmetric and hierarchic power relations, appearing virile constitutes an imperative.[9] The gaze of peers assumes a

---

[8] They often felt observed. This may explain why young Libyan men preferred to leave the country and divert themselves elsewhere, among peers exterior to their immediate peer group, see Pereira, "Les mots de la sexualité," 125.

[9] In the *Dictionnaire critique du féminisme*, Pascal Molinier & Daniel Welzer-Lang indicate that "la virilité ... est apprise et imposée aux garçons par le groupe des hommes au cours de leur socialisation pour qu'ils se distinguent hiérarchiquement des femmes. La virilité est l'expression collective et individ-

considerable importance, all the more so within a "viriarcal" society.[10] Being a virile man is inscribed in a quest of recognizing peers, and young men therefore attempt to adhere to models of virility, displaying external signs in order to forge, while exalting virile values, a reputation under the approving eye of the other members of the peer group. Virility is thus elaborated in a selfsame context, in a "virilizing confinement,"[11] put in place, at least partially, through language.

Effectively, it is the use of a certain transgressive language which allows the display of the extremely marked gender stereotypes which have the function of socializing and integrating the peer group norms. Their linguistic practices thus maintain and perpetuate masculine stereotypes and, importantly, power relations such as heteronormative masculine hegemony[12]—not only those between men and women, or masculine and feminine, but also within groups of men.

---

ualisée de la domination masculine," see Pascale Molinier and Daniel Welzer-Lang, "Féminité, Masculinité, Virilité," in *Le dictionnaire du féminisme* (Paris: PUF, 2000), 71–76. Welzer-Lang states more specifically that "[l]a virilité constitue ... l'attribut principal des hommes, des garçons, dans leurs rapports au monde, aux femmes et aux hommes, à travers les rapports sociaux de sexe. Les rapports sociaux de sexe organisent les représentations et les pratiques des hommes et des femmes en les constituant comme hommes et comme femmes dans des relations de pouvoir asymétriques et hiérarchisées, ce que Bourdieu appelle la violence symbolique," see Daniel Welzer-Lang, "Virilité et virilisme dans les quartiers populaires en France," *VEI-Enjeux* 128 (2002), 10.

[10] So-called "viriarcal" societies are societies dominated by maleness. The term "viriarcate" (French viriarcat) was proposed by Nicole-Claude Mathieu, who defines it as the power of men, whether they are fathers or not, to impose patrilinealness on society, be it patrilocal or not, see Nicole-Claude Mathieu, "Quand céder n'est pas consentir. Des déterminants matériels et psychiques de la conscience dominée des femmes, et de quelques-unes de leurs interprétations en ethnologie," in *L'Arraisonnement des Femmes. Essais en anthropologie des sexes* (Paris: EHESS, 1985), 169–245.

[11] The term comes from Guénif-Souilamas' work on young Arab men, Nacira Guénif-Souilamas, "L'enfermement viriliste: des garçons arabe plus vrais que nature," *Cosmopolitiques: Cette violence qui nous tient* 2 (2002), 47–59.

[12] See for example Judith Butler, *Gender Trouble* (London: Routledge, 1990), and Connell, *Masculinities*.

The transgressive register

The usual linguistic style of these young men, often called "youth speech", is characterized principally by the use of obscenities and sexual taboos, as well as religious taboos[13] often perceived as shocking and offensive in Muslim societies in general. Recourse to a transgressive register is characterized mainly by the omnipresence of sexual vocabulary, as can be seen in the following dialog, where numerous replies bear an exaggeratedness constructed principally by terms linked to sexuality.

A) *āne nfax, ḥayāt-i mwallya ḷ-aẓ-ẓoḅḅ, fhamt-ni?*

"I'm sick of it, my life has become shit, you feel me?"

R) *māfīš ḥadd məš nfax, ḥatta āne nfax ḷ-aẓ-ẓoḅḅ lākən əəə šən bətdīr?*

"Everyone's sick of it, me too, fucking tired of it, but hey what can you do?"

A) *āne fāhm-ək ʕlāš zmān lamma tži tūgəf baḥdā-na hekke mṭarrəm ḷ-aẓ-ẓoḅḅ, marrāt hekke, yənʕən dīn-zəkk-umm-lībya*

"Me, I understand why you used to come chill with us like that, fucking sour-faced, it's like that sometimes, curse Libya's mother's ass's religion."

R) (laughing) *yənʕən dīn-zəkk-umm-lībya...*

"(laughing) curse Libya's mother's ass's religion..."

hīya, taʕṛaf šəni tamsaḥ-ha? tamsaḥ-ha safṛa.

"You know what'll clear that up? A trip'll clear it up."

---

[13] The frequent use of taboo words is one of the main characteristics of "youth speech", cf. Jannis Androutsopoulos, "Research on Youth-Language," in *Sociolinguistics. An International Handbook of the Science of Language and Society*, ed. A. Ulrich, N. Dittmar, K. J. Mattheier, and P. Trudgill (Berlin: De Gruyter, 2005), 1499, and Anna-Brita Stenström, Gisle Andersen, and Ingrid Kristine Hasund, *Trends in Teenage Talk: Corpus Compilation, Analysis, and Findings* (Amsterdam: John Benjamins, 2002), 64–66.

A) *waḷḷāhi tamsaḥ-ha safra ḷ-aẓ-ẓobb!*

"I swear, a fucking trip'll clear it right up!"

R) *waḷḷāhi, tamsaḥ-ha safra ḷazzobb, taʕraf, təmši tnīk safra u tži talga ṛūḥ-ək mīya mīya.*

"I swear, a fucking trip'll clear it right up, you know, just go on a fucking trip and you'll come back and find yourself totally fine."

In other words, to speak in a masculine manner in Tripoli is to have recourse to a crude and obscene register of speech and to employ words related to sexuality in an exaggerated manner, which taken together reflect a certain rude and raucous comportment linked as well to the affirmation of heterosexism. This includes the recurrent usage of words referring to the male sexual organs (such as *zabb, zəbr,* or *kātsu* "penis" and *dlāwəz* "testicles"), sexual acts (*nāk-ynīk* "to fuck," *nēk* "fucking," *mnəyyək* "fucked (up)"), and prostitution (*gaḥba,* plural *ḡḥāb* "whore" and words derived from this such as *gəḥḥəb* "to be awesome" or *tgəḥḥəb* "to be pissed off"). Recourse to such taboo words allows one to perform indelicacy and rudeness. On the linguistic level, this expressiveness appears, notably, in innovative forms developed on the basis of terms of sexuality.[14]

To give an example, in the preceding dialog the term *nfax,* literally "swelling," used as a metaphor for "to be fed up," allows the expression of their discouragement and their disillusionment as they come to the conclusion that their life is pitiful: *ḥayāt-i mwallya ḷ-aẓ-ẓobb* "my life has become total shit." The term *zabb* "cock, penis" is present in this sentence in the form of an adverbial phrase *ḷ-aẓ-ẓobb,* meaning literally "to the cock" which provides vulgar emphasis to a phrase and is most effectively translated with a range of idiomatic expressions depending on the context. Then, the verb *nāk-ynīk* "to fuck" is employed as a light verb (i.e. a verb with no semantic content but which combines with an object to form an idiomatic expression) such as in the expression *tnīk safra,* literally "to fuck a trip," meaning simply "to go on a trip," or perhaps, in a corresponding vulgar register "to go on a fucking trip".

---

[14] The formation of such terms is described in Pereira, "Les mots de la sexualité."

As well, the expression *zəkk-umm* "mother's ass" is inserted between the verb *yənʕən* "to curse" and its object, permitting the expression "to curse something's ass" such as in the insult *yənʕən dīn-zəkk-umm-lībya* "curse Libya's mother's ass's religion," an expression about as taboo and vulgar as possible.

These syntactic innovations and taboo words have a transgressive function. They are used, among other things, in interaction to expressive ends: formed in the playful and humorous tone which characterizes the young men's discourse in general, these words permit the intensification of the communication. It is then in this mode and this tone that heterosexism is expressed, as the young men act it out and as they exacerbate masculine stereotypes and ultimately dominate them.

Gendered Insults

A striking example of masculine solidarity which is established by means of language is that of insults which represent the transgression of a Muslim society's particular taboos. From an axiological point of view, a pejorative or potentially degrading term is not performed as a personal insult but as a form of address.[15]

One can note two types of gendered insults: 1) certain lexical items employed as terms of address among members of a peer group which do not have the pragmatic value of an insult, and 2) insults towards social targets susceptible to being dominated, notably those whom a peer group excludes: the "puppets without virility." One can see by means of the insult that the hegemonic model of masculinity enters into conflict with, for example, alternative masculinities or masculinities considered less virile.[16]

---

[15] On pejoratives as forms of address, see Cyrille Trimaille and Océane Bois, "Adolescents et axiologie péjorative: présentation de soi et socialisation groupale," in *Les insultes en français: de la recherche fondamentale à ses applications (linguistique, littérature, histoire, droit)*, ed. D. Lagorgette (Chambéry: Université de Savoie, 2009), 113–140.

[16] David Le Breton, *Rites de virilité à l'adolescence*, (Brussels: Fédération Wallonie-Bruxelles de Belgique, 2015), 11.

Terms of address and the construction of identity

Certain insults are employed as terms of address among members of a
peer group, for example words designating "homosexual" such as *zāməl*   51
(plural *zwāməl* or *mazməl*), as well as *tēs* (plural *matyəs*) also meaning
"goat." The expressivity may be found by means of the insult.

> *mazməl ḥne mxallyīn farag̣ l-əl-kābāb ḥne zwāməl ēh!*
>
> "We are such fags for leaving some room for kebab, we're fags, yeah!"

> *fī fransa g̣ādi ya matyəs āhu ngūl l-ək ʕlāš ḍʕif anta...*
> *antu fi fransa tnīku dīma (laughs) ḥne n-nēk nəšbḥu fīh marra f-əs-sana...*
>
> "Over there in France, you fags, look I'll tell you why you're skinny.
> You in France you fuck all the time (laughs), we, we get a fuck once a
> year..."

The young men also use potentially insulting terms among themselves
in order to call or refer to each other, such as *ṣāyəʕ* "thug", *frūx-əl-
gaḥba* "son of a whore", as well as *kəlb* (plural *klāb*) "dog".

> *wēn tdūḥ ya ṣāyəʕ?*
>
> "Where are you hanging around, you thug?"

> *kāna hāda ya frūx-əl-gaḥba gāʕəd ndūr g̣ādīkāya!*
>
> "If it was like that, you son of a whore, I'd still be hanging around over
> there!"

> *wēn dāru zəkk-umm-ha, lə-klāb?*
>
> "Where have they fucking put it, the dogs?"

As they are employed here in a jesting tone used by peers to insult
each other or for self-mockery, these terms of address enter into the
construction of a social identity. For the one who employs them, they
serve to exclude those to whom they are addressed from the world
of "real" men, and thus to express domination and virility all while
maintaining group cohesion. It is precisely because they are employed
with a contrary sense, without the value of personal insult among
friends, that these expressions which seem to threaten face are actually

elements which reinforce the links of the peer group.[17]

The subjugation of the other (heterosexism)

One also finds these terms employed, in a mocking or insulting tone, in relation to the subjugation of the other. In effect, other than power and authority, competitiveness and submission, as well as toughness, the dominant mode of being a "real," heterosexual man is typically associated with subjugation, notably of homosexual men but also of women. The finding and constructing of targets who are susceptible to being discursively mocked or dominated imposes itself on the young man in order for him to prove himself as a dominant, virile male.

Therefore, all the previously mentioned words designating homosexuals are also employed as insults; to be added to these is also *mībūn* (plural *mwəbbna*) "faggot" and *bġəl* (plural *bġūla*) "mule." In the peer group, these terms also designate those who lack worth in their eyes—the association here is thus between homosexuality and worthlessness or despicableness. Speaking of someone who is rejected, in a deprecatory tone, one can hear:[18]

hāda mībūn! or *hāda bġəl!*

"That guy's a fag!"

In order to verbally provoke, certain rhyming phrases are also used by the members of the peer group. They allow a sort of humorous or playful type of insulting; these are ritualized insults, almost chanted, which allow teasing in an amplified and caricaturing manner:

ya zāməl ya tēs / naḥši l-ək būbṛēṣ
"You homo, you fag / I'll stuff a gecko (in your ass)"

ya bġəl / naḥši l-ək fi tīnt-ək təll
"You fag / I'll stick a rod up your ass"

---

[17] Trimaille & Bois, "Adolescents et axiologie péjorative."

[18] The terms *mībūn* and *bġəl* can also be used as terms of address among members of the peer group.

To be addressed as a passive homosexual is to be virulently excluded as weak from the world of "real men". Insult, and above all homophobic (and misogynistic) insult, reinforces masculine domination and the cult of virility.[19] Additionally, hegemonic models of masculinity enter into conflict with other masculinities considered to be less virile. On this topic, the below phrase, uttered by a young man in Tripoli annoyed after realizing that others were mocking him for being effeminate, shows that the criteria of virility are not always the same from person to person or group to group.

> *tašbḫū-ni hēkke təḥsābū-ni mā-nnīk-š? waḷḷāhi nnīk-kum wāḥəd wāḥəd!*
>
> "You see me like that? You think I don't fuck? I swear, I'll fuck all of you one by one!"

This young man challenges here those who consider themselves "real men": challenging them that he will prove his virility, and confirm physically his ability to be sexually dominant, by means of the erect and penetrating form which characterizes the virile masculine sexuality expressed by the verb *nnīk* "I fuck."[20] In the discourse of young men, the affirmation of virility and heterosexuality—linked to contempt of the other, especially homosexuals, effeminate men, those considered to be lacking worth and thus contemptible—has, in Libyan society, the monopoly on legitimate sexuality. Heterosexism thus appears as a sort of "gender policing" intended to remind one of the symbolic order and thus confirm masculine domination in relationships between the sexes.

Heterosexuality reclaimed

Sexuality allows the performance of virility. It is in effect by his sex and his sexual activity that the young man becomes aware of his identity and his virility; sexual activity which affirms his heterosexuality to other

---

[19] Welzer-Lang, "Virilité et virilisme dans les quartiers populaires en France," 19.

[20] The verb *nāk-ynīk* "to fuck, have sex with (actively)" contrasts with the derived verb *tnāk-yətnāk* "to be fucked, to be the passive sexual partner."

members of the peer group. It being the case that young Libyan women should be virgins when they marry, young heterosexual Libyan men who desire sexual relations have few options other than prostitutes (or perhaps non-Libyan women). There were in fact paid forms of sexual service which these young men could take advantage of, as discussed for example in the following dialog:

54

A) *fi ghāb az̧-z̧ab̬b fi ma nnīku z̧-z̧ab̬b?*

"Are there some fucking prostitutes? Is there something to fuck?"

B) *āmta tawwa?*

"When, now?"

A) *ti ēh...*

"Yea, of course..."

B) *fi wāḥda swēla*

"There's a dark (woman)"

A) *bāh! mlīḥa?*

"Alright! Is she fine?"

B) *təbbī-ha?*

"Do you want her?"

A) *ʕādi!*

"Fine!"

B) *b-əl-flūs lākən ṛā-h!*

"But you have to pay, you know!"

In this dialog, one can see both how virility and domination are performed by means of a kind of sexuality. In this context, having recourse only to prostitution in order to fornicate, a symbol of virility. The young men's representation of the sexual act (outside of marriage) almost approaches a pornographic practice.

From the first phrase of the dialog above, one sees that interlocutor

A asks for "prostitutes" (*ghāb*), a term through which a certain relationship of domination is expressed: the notion of domination appears in the context of prostitution in the figure of the one who has money and pays for the service. Then, without transition and in the same phrase, the interlocutor asks if there is "something to fuck" (*fi ma nnīku?*)—the relative pronoun *ma* is used for objects, not persons, in which case the expression would be "someone to fuck" (*fi man nnīku?*). One thus observes the devalorization and subsequent reification of the prostitute; representing her as a sexual object allows heterosexism, domination, and virility to be expressed in a context in which, obsessed by their virility, young men do not really consider their sexual organs as ones of pleasure but rather as tools: the instruments of performance. [21] Then, as the dialog continues, their sexual comportment is presented as crude and also brutal: they speak of "shooting" a prostitute, using the English word "shoot," in the phrase *tšūt-ha* "you shoot her."

A)   *ēh, bāh! swēla, ʕbēda, mlīḥa wlla nafəx?*

        "Yeah, okay! Brown, black, is she pretty or is this a dumb plan?"

B)   *swēla! la, la mlīḥa*

        "Brown! No, no, she's pretty."

A)   *ṣangṭa?*

        "A bombshell?"

B)   *la, la, məš ṣangṭa, mlīḥa žisəm-ha bāhi lākən tugʕud fī-k ṣannət-əs-swēlāt əl-gaḥba baʕd-ma tšūt-ha* (laughs)

        "No, no, not a bombshell (but) she's pretty, has a nice body, but damn the smell of dark women stays with you after you've shot her (laughs)."

A)   *āh!*

        "Ah!"

---

[21] Elisabeth Badinter, *XY, de l'identité masculine* (Paris: Odile Jacob, 1992), 204.

B)   *ʕrəft-ha ṣannət-əs-swēlāt? lākən š-šʕaṛ š-šʕaṛ əl-məlwi...*

"You know it, the smell of dark (women)? But the hair, the curly hair..."

A)   *hmmm...hmmm...!*

"Hm, hm"

B)   *lə-ʕyūn mlowwnāt, ʕyūn-ha mlowwnāt xuḍur*

"The eyes are colored, her eyes are green colored"

A)   *l-gaḥba!*

"Damn!"

B)   *uqsum billāh u šwāṛəb ʕənd-ha mlāḥ l-az-ẓaḅḅ...*

"I swear to God, and she has damn nice lips..."

At no time are sensuality or eroticism expressed; sentiments and affection are, in these stereotypes, associated with women and would be interpreted as unvirile. These sexual practices are therefore disassociated from sentiments of affection. Nevertheless, interlocutor B converses in a less abstract manner, describing the prostitute's physical attributes mostly positively: she has a "good body" (*žisəm-ha bāhi*), "curly hair" (*š-šʕaṛ əl-məlwi*), "green eyes" (*ʕyūn-ha mlowwnāt xuḍur*), and "damn nice lips" (*šwāṛəb ʕənd-ha mlāḥ l-az-ẓaḅḅ*)—these details allow him to imply that he already knows her sexually, has perhaps already had relations with her, and that he is thus an active and accomplished heterosexual. This is reinforced by the insulting and racist comment that he adds, noting that after the sexual act he could still sense a "smell of dark women" (*ṣannət-əs-swēlāt*). Thus B expresses his virility while showing off, while also putting himself into the scene and bragging, boastfulness being as well a characteristic of young men employed in dominating and obtaining the recognition of peers.[22]

Setting the scene of a gendered self

---

[22] See Coates, *Men Talk*.

The staging of the self takes place above all in the narrations through which masculine identity and virility are performed. This is primarily via the choice of insults and taboo words as well as via the narrating of one's exploits—be they sexual, violent, or connected to alcohol consumption—wherein a virile comportment, considered to be masculine, is foregrounded.[23] This may be observed in the following extracts. In the first extract, interlocutor C recounts his plans to travel outside of Libya for a few days in order to drink and live without responsibilities. A trip such as that would give him an access to leisure activities he would not be able to achieve in Libya:

C)   *b-nəmši wullāhi ngūl l-ək ḥāža m-əl-āxīr?*
         b-nəmši nəskər u b-nasraḥ ʕale ṛūḥ-i hekke
         sbūʕēn tlāta u bə-nrawwaḥ...

         "I intend to go, I swear, I'm talking to you
         seriously, huh? I'll go and get drunk and just
         have fun, like that, two, three weeks, and then
         I'll come back..."

D)   *ēh!*
         "Yeah!"

C)   *sukrān hekke fāqəd tlāt sābīʕ u xlāṣ...*
         "Drunk, just like that, three weeks wasted and
         that's it..."

D)   (laughs)

C)   *m-əl-āxīr...*
         "Seriously..."

This interlocutor fantasizes by means of an imaginary trip allowing him to stage himself: he transports himself outside of Libya, where he is able to lose control. Virility is expressed by means of the exploit which he will accomplish once there: getting drunk. A dialog such as this is in essence a playful exercise which permits, in a humorous tone, the centering of attention, boasting, and domination. This may also be seen in another dialog, below, where interlocutor E recounts an

---

[23] Ibid.

encounter which upset him. The exploits which are foregrounded are drunkenness and verbal violence directed towards another young man.

E) *taʕṛaf wāḥəd hāḍāka l-maṛṛa fi lēla sukṛān əl-mudda lli fātət u nāk ttaṣṣəl nnīk, ttaṣṣəl gult āne ālō, sakkəṛ, nnīk nabʕat l-a māsəž, ma-fī-hā-š kaləmtēn mūfīdāt f-žurrət baʕḍ-hum*

"You know, a guy, that one time, I was drunk one night, a while ago, and he fucking called me, dammit, he called and I said 'hello', he hung up. So I send him a fucking message without even two words that make sense in it..."

F) *w ənta sukṛān?*

"And you were drunk?"

E) *mā-fī-hā-š kalma mā-fī-hā-š sabba!*

"There wasn't a word that wasn't a curse!"

F) *w ənta sukṛān?*

"And you were drunk?"

E) *ēh u kull-a fak fak fak fak fak fak fak fak yu wen yu kōl ðə fakiŋ fakiŋ fakiŋ, yu dont hæŋ əp ðə fakiŋ fōn yu dont fakiŋ fakiŋ fakiŋ fakiŋ kōl, āy kallamt-a ma-bā-š iṛudd fhamt-ni?*

"Yeah and it was all [English] 'fuck fuck fuck fuck fuck fuck fuck fuck you when you call the fucking fucking fucking you don't hang up the fucking phone you don't fucking fucking fucking fucking call', yea, I called him and he wouldn't respond, you got me?"

F) *ēh!*

"Yeah!"

E) *nnīk l-a māsəž...*

"I send him a fucking message..."

F) *māsəž kull-a fakiŋ*

"A message (where) it is all fucking"

Contrary to the preceding dialog, here interlocutor E has recourse only to a crude form of language, obscene and full of insults. He speaks aggressively. He sets himself in a kind of telephone brawl where he dominates the other via insults. Virility, domination, and boastfulness are all on display. Domination also appears via the monopoly of speech, as a way of prevailing in a peer group. Here it can be seen that E dominates F by blocking his interventions, interrupting him, and not listening to his words. These masculine performances are homosocial, and this *mise-en-scène* permits one to obtain the recognition of peers. The chosen themes allow one to choose how one presents and shows oneself, how one wants to appear, themes which play an important role in identity construction.[24]

Conclusions

Through these unguarded, spontaneous oral conversations, gathered *in situ* directly within the peer group, one may begin to comprehend the ways in which the linguistic habit of young Tripolitanian men indeed performs traditional, stereotyped, and hegemonic masculinities through virile comportments, to use the terminology of Kiesling.[25] The exalting of virilist values and foregrounding of heterosexism through transgressive, very obscene, highly expressive, language practices, express an identity constrained by traditional society and a lack of a certain kind of sexual freedom. The reproduction of hegemonic models of masculinity allows young men to perform domination, toughness, and insensitivity in order to distinguish themselves from women while reaffirming each other. This virility materializes via the discursive affirmation of a measured, heterosexual sexuality outside of marriage, humor consisting of gendered insults and a strong homophobic tendency, and a self-presentation, all of which define an important part of homosocialness, whereas the expression of power appears constantly via sexist and homophobic utterances, where women and homosexuals are constructed as being "others" inferior to the members of the peer group. This construction of a social identity, exercised sometimes through self-ridicule, other times in order to subjugate the "other," thus permits these young men to validate their existence as dominant males. While assigned a particular identity imposed by the

---

[24] See again Coates, *Men Talk*.

[25] Kiesling, "Men, Masculinities and Language," 657.

social conditions which constrain them, it is interesting to note that their language practices aim to emancipate them from the constraints in which they live while they simultaneously reproduce the expected, dominant, imposed comportments. What is then lived as transgressive or even emancipatory serves stereotyped categories, which, far from participating in an intimate sexual identity, one both chosen and personal, encloses each person in preconceived frameworks.

Bibliography

Androutsopoulos, Jannis. "Research on Youth-Language." In *Sociolinguistics. An International Handbook of the Science of Language and Society*, edited by A. Ulrich, N. Dittmar, K. J. Mattheier, and P. Trudgill, 1496–1505. Berlin: De Gruyter, 2005.

Arnett, Jeffrey. "Emerging Adulthood. A Theory of Development. From the Late Teens Through the Twenties." *American Psychologists*, 55/5 (2000), 469–480.

Badinter, Elisabeth. *XY, de l'identité masculine*. Paris: Odile Jacob, 1992.

Butler, Judith. *Gender Trouble*. London: Routledge, 1990.

Cameron, Deborah. "Gender, Language and Discourse: A Review Essay." *Signs* 23 (1998), 945–973.

Coates, Jennifer. *Men Talk. Stories in the Making of Masculinities*. Malden: Blackwell Publishing, 2003.

Connell, Raewyn. *Masculinities*. Berkeley: University of California Press, 2005.

Guénif-Souilamas, Nacira. "L'enfermement viriliste: des garçons arabe plus vrais que nature." *Cosmopolitiques: Cette violence qui nous tient* 2 (2002), 47–59.

Kiesling, Scott. "Men, Masculinities and Language." *Blackwell Linguistics and Language Compass* 1/6 (2007), 653–673.

Le Breton, David. *Rites de virilité à l'adolescence*. Brussels: Fédération Wallonie-Bruxelles de Belgique, 2015.

Mathieu, Nicole-Claude. "Quand céder n'est pas consentir. Des déterminants matériels et psychiques de la conscience dominée des femmes, et de quelques-unes de leurs interprétations en ethnologie." In *L'Arraisonnement des Femmes. Essais en anthropologie des sexes*, edited by N-C. Mathieu, 169–245. Paris: EHESS, 1985.

Moïse, Claudine, Christophe Pereira, Ángeles Vicente, and Karima Ziamari. "La construction socio-langagière du genre: jeunes hommes libyens, jeunes femmes marocaines et rapport à la masculinité." In *Sociolinguistique des pratiques langagières de jeunes*, edited by C. Trimaille, C. Pereira, K. Ziamari, and M. Gasquet-Cyrus, 81–115. Grenoble: UGA Éditions, 2020.

Molinier, Pascale & Daniel Welzer-Lang. "Féminité, Masculinité, Virilité." In *Le dictionnaire du féminisme*, 71–76. Paris: PUF, 2000.

61

Pereira, Christophe. *Le parler arabe de Tripoli (Libye)*. Zaragoza: IEIOP, 2010.

62

Pereira, Christophe. "Les mots de la sexualité dans l'arabe de Tripoli (Libye): désémantisation, grammaticalisation et évolution linguistique." In *L'Année du Maghreb. Numéro VI. Dossier: Sexualités au Maghreb: Essais d'ethnographies contemporaines*, edited by V. Beaumont, C. Cauvin Verner & F. Pouillon, 117–140. Paris: CNRS Editions, 2010.

Stenström Anna-Brita, Gisle Andersen, and Ingrid Kristine Hasund. *Trends in Teenage Talk Corpus compilation, analysis and findings*. Amsterdam: John Benjamins, 2002.

Trimaille, Cyrille & Océane Bois. "Adolescents et axiologie péjorative: présentation de soi et socialisation groupale." In *Les insultes en français: de la recherche fondamentale à ses applications (linguistique, littérature, histoire, droit)*, edited by D. Lagorgette. 113–140. Chambéry: Université de Savoie, 2009.

Welzer-Lang, Daniel. "Virilité et virilisme dans les quartiers populaires en France." *VEI-Enjeux* 128 (2002), 10–32.

Tasnim Qutait

Retracing a Disappearing Landscape: On Libyan Cultural Memory

WHAT DOES IT MEAN TO SPEAK OF LIBYAN CULTURAL MEMORY? What museums should we visit, what archives should we consult, what oral histories and material artefacts should we gather, to begin to tell the stories of Libya? The exhibition "Retracing A Disappearing Landscape," held at the P21 Gallery in London, and running for six weeks between March and May 2018, was a rare opportunity to explore these questions. The exhibition, curated by Najlaa Elageli, set out to showcase "people's direct experience of and fascination with memory and personal history as well as the collective narratives that arise in connection with modern day Libya." Alongside the exhibition, there was a parallel programme of talks by artists, writers and academics, including novelist Najwa Bin Shatwan, poets Khaled Mattawa and Farrah Fray, and director Jihan Kikhia, as well as academics Adam Benkato and Barbara Spadaro, and Adam Styp-Rekowski and Guy Martin discussing their photographs of Tripoli and Benghazi respectively.

More than a century ago, Maurice Halbwachs defined memory as a social phenomenon. In recent years, the interest in cultural memory and in heritage has been described as a memory industry, often critiqued as an over-personalizing of history, interlinked with centering trauma and victimization. Kerwin Lee Klein has argued that "one of the reasons for memory's sudden rise is that it promises to let us have our essentialism and deconstruct it, too." To speak of cultural memory is to speak of history that belongs to us, as Jan Assman puts it, memory as knowledge with "an identity index." Essentialism is entangled in the questions we ask and the stories we tell ourselves about where we come from and who we are. Who do we include, and who do we exclude, when we draw the boundaries around our ethnic, national, cultural and religious identities?

During the Qaddafi regime, billboards across Libya were plastered with a ubiquitous map of a dark jagged territory shining a benevolent light down onto the African continent. This image seemed curiously apropos, representing the country as a missing puzzle piece, spotlighting its own absence in narratives outside of itself. In the regime narrative, Libya was the beacon of enlightened thought extending its rays across the global south, but in reality it seemed to figure as the blank, an enigma, a hyphen between the swathe of countries that had been consolidated as the Maghrib and the Mashriq. In the last years of the regime, Libya was hardly mentioned on the Arabic-speaking news, while mention of the country would only rarely appear on the Western media, mostly in relation to Lockerbie reparations, to migration routes, or, after the Iraq invasion, to surrendering weapons, to the rapprochement, Tony Blair earnestly shaking hands with Qaddafi under the patterned tent.

Since the 2011 revolution and the subsequent years of conflict, we have entered an age in which we are confronted on a daily basis with a cascade of images and narratives through social media, new narratives that sediment and press down what happened only days before in what feels like an ever-accelerating process. In this time of civil strife, the notion of cultural memory might seem a luxury, a nostalgic yearning. Yet Astrid Erll argues that it is precisely at times of crisis that "we cannot afford the luxury of not studying memory," since we need to examine "paradigms that were formed in long historical processes [...] to understand the different ways in which people handle time, and this refers not only to their 'working through the past', but also includes their understanding of the present and visions for the future." As Edward Said also puts it, "[m]emory and its representations touch very significantly upon questions of identity, of nationalism, of power and authority." The fragmentations and the faultlines within Libyan society today speak to the urgency of grappling with the historical processes that have led us here, not least in order to imagine how alternative visions of a national identity might be formulated for the future.

The *Retracing A Disappearing Landscape* exhibition gathered work by over twenty artists, related in various ways to preserving and reflecting on cultural and national memory, ranging from oral narratives and projects drawing on and responding to family photo albums, to paintings and contemporary pieces reacting to the post-2011 context. The title of the exhibition was well-chosen: the concept of the trace suggests something whose presence marks an absence, while to retrace what is disappearing, fading from view, suggests an effort at guessing, following back, which is recurrent and repeated and never resolved. The relatively small exhibition space meant that the various installations jostled against each other, a mixing of visual and aural and tactile, tapestries hanging over paintings, archival photographs next to physical objects, installations in conversation and juxtaposition.

Perhaps the most immediate sense of the disappearance of heritage was represented in the woven patterns of tapestry and folkloric arts, standing in the exhibition space as a testament to fading artforms and local traditions. More literal disappearances were explored in other instances, including work on the missing, those who disappeared during the revolution, in work by Guy Martin entitled *The Missing: Re-Photographed;* the "re" signifying that these are photographs of posters with the missings' names and faces. Amidst the artistic and cultural production, to see this installation brought back sharply the disorienting realization that Libya had become a place to which journalists come from afar to photograph violence. No matter how normal this fact becomes, it will never be normal. The installation brought into focus too the fragmentary nature of the news discourse: the photographs of posters were stories on pause, moments in time. Where do we go to find the rest of the story? Who has kept the records?

Another disappearance appeared in an installation by Marcella Mameli-Badi, Alla Budabbus, and Taqwa Barnosa centered on the Ghazala statue in Tripoli. This statue of a woman and a gazelle, a landmark of the city and a marker of the colonial past, "disappeared" in 2014. In the installation, a triptych of images reimagine this disappearance, with words on the images reflecting on its loss. Do we read this disappearance as a sign of the puritanical forces that seek to selectively form cultural experience? Should we mourn the disappearance of the statue, and if we do mourn it, how do we reconcile that sense of loss with the pervasive, problematic nostalgia for colonialism against the melancholy of a seemingly never-ending postcolonial hangover?

The nostalgic object was a common theme in the exhibition, from Laila Sharif's *Dearest To Me*, which incorporated archives with family photographs, to the nostalgically familiar embroidered pillowcases in Reem Gibriel's work, *In Sense of Remembrance*, which were intended to "highlights the sense of smell as part of many shared memories that linger in the consciousness." Gibriel describes the "self-deception" of nostalgia, but also the way in which it "allows us to draw strength from memory," and relates the power of "long[ing] for something that no longer exists but that defines our sense of belonging." While Gibriel's work focused on smell, Malak Elghwel's video collage *Mendar* brought aspects of cultural memory to life, including snippets of the popular show *Besbasi*. These are works which spoke to the theme of reinterpreting what is disappearing and making sense of what remains. According to Erll, again, this is the "critical potential to nostalgia" which "keeps constructions of a 'past future' alive and measures them against the present." The memory is less about the past than the active and constant reconstruction of the past in the present and for the future.

Svetlana Boym describes nostalgia as working through the "superimposition of two images – of home and abroad, past and present, dream and everyday life," a superimposition Boym describes through the "cinematic image" of a "double exposure." This method shaped Jihan Kikhia's moving documentary film, *Finding Kikhia*, on the disappearance of the director's father, which interwove family video of Mansur Kikhia with news footage, capturing the need to return again and again to the images that remain, and which carry the emotional weight of an inability to mourn. Kikhia's exploration of disappearance and its psychological shadow connects with the work of the novelist Hisham Matar, who has explored his own father's disappearance in literary form in *The Return: Fathers, Sons and the Land In Between* (2016). Both Kikhia and Matar interweave life in the shadow of this unresolved personal tragedy with the 2011 revolution, an ending of the regime which does not provide a resolution for the lingering effects of what the regime inflicted over its forty years.

In *The Return*, Hisham Matar writes about the fact that there are few modern histories of Libya, and those that are available are often written by outsiders. Matar concludes that this dearth of historical accounts means that "to be Libyan is to live with questions." *Retracing A Disappearing Landscape* sought not to bring resolution to these questions, but to explore what it means to grapple with the absence of answers, now and into the future.

HADIA GANA

Building Bayt Ali Gana

DURING THE JAMAHIRIYYA (1969-2011), Libya was under "emergency law" and assembly was forbidden. In this way, all possibilities for constructive exchange between citizens, cultural spaces, and public spaces were reduced to a minimum. Toward the end of the 1990s foundations appeared, but these all had to be under the umbrellas of either the Qaddafi International Charity and Development Foundation or Aisha Qaddafi's charitable foundation. During the first year of the post-revolution period, hundreds of NGOs and socio-cultural institutions were registered, encouraged by the transitional ministry of culture. However, since then, the majority have vanished or struggle to exist. Most lacked long-term vision and planning in their initial formation. The country's inhabitants suffer from traumas left by four decades of destabilization; more recently this is emphasized by the polarization of different ideological and political tendencies, continuing the destructive process. What features and strategies could cultural spaces embody to create a sustainable environment propitious for dialogue and freedom of thought and movement?

In this essay I trace the emergence of four Libyan cultural institutions after 2011. I place my own ongoing experience building Bayt Ali Gana in context alongside the examples of Tanarout and Habka in Benghazi and WaraQ in Tripoli. How can cultural spaces create environments for dialogue, negotiation, and creative thinking, thereby helping to relieve traumatic stress disorders on a broad social scale?

Eight years after the end of the 2011 revolution and death of Libya's former leader, the country under consecutive weak governments now counts two governments with negligible effective power and continues to undergo mini-wars bursting here and there, erratic, emphasizing the sense of insecurity and instability, enhancing secular divisions and enlarging the void between communities. Strangely, those problems are in a way dealt with by a population moving "nomadically" from one city to another or from an area to another. However, their daily repercussions are the heaviest to bear for most. Those boomerang effects are constant: extremely long power cuts, blackouts, water cuts, drastic monetary inflation, and shortages of local currency in the banks paralyzing the whole country.

Statistics in general, and certainly those related to culture, continue to be scant for Libya. Although Libya is now a more democratic environment than during the dictatorial era, political polarization, armed conflict, and remnants of imbued distrust make it an unstable environment where it can be difficult to observe the work of small and medium sized cultural activities for external reporting. A report published by DIGNITY: Danish Institute Against Torture in October 2014, concludes that:

> both the short-term consequences of the internal conflict as well as the long-term consequences of the Qaddafi regime are in large measures still unaddressed. In order to deal with life stress, 59% [of people interviewed] indicated they needed assistance in terms of justice, legal remedy and compensation, while 44% indicated they needed health and medical assistance. Thus, the report concludes that any future government of Libya faces massive challenges in alleviating human suffering and improving mental health. However, as the internal conflict continues more and more people are affected by human rights violations aggravating mental health afflictions, straining the social fabric and the capacity of the Libyan state.[1]

This survey can be seen as a rough sketch of the situation; other surveys should follow with more accurate data specifying the groups targeted (socially and geographically). Alarming as it is, this report helps illustrate the need for safe spaces for gathering and discussion, places where people interact with each other far from political or ideological conflicts and learn to find links among each other that are not family- or job-related.

---

[1]   Fathi Ali, Morten Koch Andersen, Ahlam Chemlali, Jens Modvig, Mette Skar, and Henrik Ronsbo, "Consequences of Torture and Organized Violence: Libya Needs Assessment Survey," DIGNITY: Danish Institute Against Torture, 14 October 2014, www.temehu.com/HOR/dignity-report-torture-and-mental-health-in-libya.pdf (accessed 21 May 2019).

For this reason, I will describe the paths of three Libyan cultural institutions that materialized after 2011—WaraQ, Tanarout, and Habka—before concluding with a discussion of my own project, Bayt Ali Gana. This enables me to give an overview of some common challenges Libyan cultural institutions have faced in the post-2011 environment and recount the resourceful responses of these institutions' founders to these challenges.

The first, WaraQ,[2] was initiated in 2016 by Tewa Barnosa, then 17 years old, with the support of her parents. She created a multidisciplinary space to answer her own need for a shared art studio where young creatives could meet, work, discuss, learn from each other, and encourage each other. WaraQ was a much-needed space, well-situated in the city center. Discussions were organized, themed exhibitions flirting with a conceptual approach to curatorial work started to appear, young digital artists were exhibited, and an interesting buzzing creative ecosystem started to flourish. Like other art activities in Libya, they started with a WaraQ Art Community group on Facebook in which young art lovers and artists would post their work, slowly building greater interest and popularity. The physical space materialized in a rented basement that they redesigned and furnished in the international trend of reuse and minimal design, taking a bright yellow as their brand color. After approximately one year of existence, the landlord changed his mind and interrupted the contract rather aggressively with the excuse that the space encouraged young people of both genders to mix and that it wasn't "correct religiously and socially". This abrupt end of contract came with no compensation. After a few months recovering from the shock, Tewa continued on her path. This experience matured her view on curatorial activities and she decided to exhibit young Libyan artists abroad while teaching herself Arabic calligraphy and using the internet to build international connections, network, and research. However, traveling with the artists' works under her arms in order to exhibit – with the current situation (there are no foreign embassies at which to apply for visas in Libya, obliging everybody to transit via Tunisia, Egypt, or Turkey using devaluated Libyan currency) revealed itself to be an excessively heavy weight on her shoulders, so she reduced her pace and turned to local public space

---

[2]   https://waraqartfoundation.com/

as galleries, organizing a series of exhibitions, screenings, discussions in the Old City of Tripoli under the name "Art Out, The City is Our Gallery." WaraQ is now an art foundation with more than fourteen thousand cyber followers aiming to create environments propitious to creativity in Libya and the region.

The second cultural organization is Tanarout.[3] The initiators of this space are of a middle-aged generation of artists. They worked on various cultural activities and organized exhibitions during the pre-revolution era. With this experience, Tanarout thus blossomed after 2011 to become a multidisciplinary center offering drawing and painting classes, music classes, cultural discussions, and poetry readings, among other events. The space evolved as a club, with partners, memberships, and adherents. The first space was situated in Benghazi's city center, a rented flat on the ground floor that they had to flee after having been threatened several times by fundamentalists. They then decided to move to the outskirts of the city, into a larger venue that they left as an open space, inviting young artists to inhabit the space with their artwork and organizing artistic events grouping music, fine arts, and creative writing. The classes offered evolve depending on the members' availability and willingness to give classes.

The third institution is a cyber platform: a network of cartoonists linked together by mangaka Abdullah Hadia and script-writer Alhouni. The buddies started working on their own projects after 2011, showing their work on different social media platforms, thus gaining an audience and adherents. They then decided to create a Libyan manga magazine that would gather the work of young Libyan cartoonists. To do that, they received funding and organized a series of workshops to gather the creatives and let them meet and work together on specific tasks such as a "one page story". The participants work remotely, independently, and send their work to be published in Habka magazine,[4] which is then distributed in limited print editions as well digitally. Even if they have no stable place to meet, Habka creators regularly organize workshops in rented spaces and enlarge their network through the different social media platforms.

I strongly believe that culture and arts can play an essential mediating role and help to relieve the traumas affecting people and which, if not tackled, will continue to spread through generations.

---

[3] https://www.facebook.com/TanaroutLy/

[4] http://www.habkamagazine.com/

Stress, lack of concentration, lack of trust, difficulty in dialogue, instability, and an inability to plan long-term are some of the PTSD symptoms that have to be fought with all means possible to reconstruct a society, a country. Bayt Ali Gana[5] aims to give a little push in that direction. It is a cultural center based on the collections and studies of a Libyan artist who had a unique position in being multi-disciplinary and transgenerational. Ali Gana (1936-2006) is usually presented as one of the first-generation artists in modern Libya. He graduated from the Scuola degli Belle Arti in Rome in the early 1960s and went back home to teach in Tripoli's Faculty of Architecture from 1970 to 2002. Besides teaching, he sketched, collected, photographed, and studied local crafts and architecture. Ali Gana has the potential to be a reconciliatory figure as he was respected, trusted, and known to be a pleasant interlocutor and listener. Following the same path, the cultural space named after him is planned to be social and educational. The project also came into existence after the 2011 Libyan revolution, surfing the opening that the country witnessed after forty years of prohibition. The Bayt Ali Gana project is to me a work in progress, as even though the aim or end result is designed, it has a wide spectrum of input possibilities by friends of the project, causing it to grow slowly but steadily in a country that has been accustomed to abrupt decisions changing drastically from one day to the next.

The preparation stage of the cultural house was executed underground, with only very few people knowing about it. The main response at that time (2012-2014) when I said that I was planning to create a museum in the name of my father was always along the lines of "this is not the right time for a museum...wait a bit for the country to settle." To me that was exactly the right time to start a community/cultural project of which I would be the first beneficiary, as I needed to create a project to keep me busy and positive during a long period of time. I wanted a project that would be able to evolve gradually depending on the country's circumstances, in a protected environment, with quasi no budget to start with. The Bayt Ali Gana cultural space is a two-floor private house situated in Tripoli's outskirts. The building is Ali Gana's family house designed and built by the artist himself with his friend Professor Kamal Kaabazi during the 1970s. The building is not vast, but has all the potential to host an exhibition area to become the collection showroom on the first floor. On the ground floor and in the garden is a multidisciplinary space, a cafe, toilet facilities, and an

---

[5]   https://www.facebook.com/ali.ganafoundation/

iron extension which was designed to host a rooftop library, add more exhibition space on the first floor, and cover a lobby/winter garden on the ground floor.

The first step after the decision was to completely vacate it and build partitions to separate the private area from the public areas and a room prepared to host the artist collection and be the archive of the Bayt. The second stage needed a specialized workforce and knowledge to restore parts of the building and create new openings. I contacted a friend and student of my father, the architect Izat Khairy, seeking a professional viewpoint to change the first-floor setting, create new openings, remove walls, and redo deteriorated areas of the building. The response was an immediate boost of energy that worked both ways and the work started in 2014, just after a major armed clash burst in Tripoli, during a period in which kidnappings for ransoms flourished and the atmosphere was tense. Around this time the country's electricity plants started showing major failures as their long overdue backups could not be finished due to the instability, and extremely long power cuts became the norm. The few hours of electricity each day were awaited like a water drop in the desert and, as bad news never comes alone, water would stop flowing in areas fed by the governmental water system as the pumps started collapsing. The citizens needing water from wells drilled in their gardens, needed energy to extract the water, and started buying generators, adding to the different layers of stress with noise; and of course, generators just like cars need petrol to work, and that also became scarce due to several reasons mostly related to corruption. Despite that, work on the Bayt continued day by day.

Since 2015 the project has evolved before its potential makers and customers. Similar to a reality show, the Bayt Ali Gana project keeps a daily dairy posted on Facebook explaining the "work of the day" in Libyan dialect and with photos or time-lapses, pointing out the different stages of work, joking about the difficulties and solutions that it is going through. Like soap operas that last for years and become part of the family, this diary is usually posted at the end of the day, and has become for some followers a routine to be checked. Some started asking for visits through private messages; others asked how they could help. Could they take part by either giving money or a helping hand? Through the page I ask for advice, encouraging followers to take active steps in building and preparing the space, thus creating a sense of inclusivity often lost. The cultural platform is a collaborative project. It reaches out for solutions but waits for potential helpers to come once they decide or feel the real need to give a hand. Forcing their way in, appropriating it yet understanding that the space is a private and community nucleus. In the future, it will collaborate with different local institutions such as Arete, the Libyan Board of Architecture, WaraQ, and Tanarout, among others. Artists, designers and architects are naturally participating in the making of the Bayt and when the environment is ready, it will seek cooperation with international institutions to exchange knowledge, experience, and widen its field.

I think of Bayt Ali Gana as a low-threshold environment, a vivarium in which ways to induce curiosity for culture are studied. Ali Gana had a wide range of interests encompassing art, architecture, design, crafts, and environment. The eclectic collection and archive he left behind will be the core of the center's program. Discussions, debates, workshops will be designed as part of that. Finally, the name *bayt* ("house") was chosen for its symbolism, a protective space to feel safe enough to behave "naturally," educate, and boost the will to participate and share creative thoughts.

André Naffis-Sahely

"The Whole Shadow of Man": Alessandro Spina's Libyan Epic

THREE MONTHS AFTER ALESSANDRO SPINA'S DEATH in July 2013, Ilario Bertoletti, his Italian editor, published a memoir where he described his first near-encounter with the notoriously reclusive writer: "It was June, 1993. The bell rang in the late afternoon; moments later, a colleague entered my office: 'A gentleman dropped by. He looked like an Arab prince, tall and handsome. He left a history of the Maronites for you.'" The editor made some enquiries and discovered that Spina had been quietly publishing a number of novels and short stories since the early 1960s which charted the history of Libya from 1911, when Italy had invaded the sleepy Ottoman province, all the way to 1966, when petrodollars sparked an economic boom, exacerbating the corruption and nepotism that eventually paved the way for Muammar Qaddafi's coup d'état in 1969. It took Bertoletti, who runs an independent imprint based in Brescia, fifteen years to persuade Spina to let him reissue his books, or rather to assemble them into a 1250-page omnibus edition entitled *I confini dell'ombra: in terra d'oltremare / The Confines of the Shadow: In Lands Overseas* (Morcelliana, 2007), a cycle comprising six novels, a novella and four collections of stories, which Spina, who'd only settled on a definitive structure and title in 2003, summarized thus:

> The sequence of novels and short stories takes as its subject the Italian experience in Cyrenaica. *The Young Maronite* (1971) discusses the 1911 war prompted by Giolitti, *Omar's Wedding* (1973) narrates the ensuing truce and the attempt by the two peoples to strike a compromise before the rise of Fascism. *The Nocturnal Visitor* (1979) chronicles the end of the twenty-year Libyan resistance; *Officers' Tales* (1967) focuses on the triumph of colonialism – albeit this having been achieved when the end of Italian hegemony already loomed in sight and the Second World War appeared inevitable – and *The Psychological Comedy* (1992), which ends with Italy's

retreat from Libya and the fleeing of settlers. *Entry into Babylon* (1976) concentrates on Libyan independence in 1951, *Cairo Nights* (1986) illustrates the early years of the Senussi Monarchy and the looming spectre of Pan-Arab nationalism, while *The Shore of the Lesser Life* (1997) examines the profound social and political changes that occurred when large oil and gas deposits were discovered in the mid 1960s. Each text can be read independently or as part of the sequence. Either mode of reading will produce different – but equally legitimate – impressions.

A year later, *The Confines of the Shadow* was unanimously awarded the Premio Bagutta, Italy's highest literary accolade. It was an impressive achievement, especially for an author who'd insisted on publishing his books in limited editions with tiny outfits, all of which had fallen out of print by the early 1990s. However, the Bagutta nod only caused a faint ripple: a single radio interview, a handful of glowing reviews and a conference in his honor, which he didn't attend. Lacking a persona to grapple onto—the back flap doesn't even feature a photograph—the book receded into obscurity, and although Spina remains little known even in Italy, where he spent the last thirty years of his life, The Confines of the Shadow belongs alongside panoptic masterpieces like *Buddenbrooks*, *The Man Without Qualities*, and *The Cairo Trilogy*.

Spina died two weeks before I concluded an agreement with a London publisher to translate the entirety of *The Confines of the Shadow*. Denied the privilege to meet him, I was faced with a conundrum: the translation of such a monumental opus in the immediate wake of the author's death meant any afterword I produced would have to deal with his life, of which I knew next to nothing, save that 'Alessandro Spina' was a nom de plume adopted in 1955 when Alberto Moravia published his first story, 'L'ufficiale' / 'The Officer' in *Nuovi Argomenti*. Sporting an English reticence and safely ensconced behind his pseudonym, Spina had spent half a century eluding the limelight, refusing invitations to make public appearances or to concede interviews. Consequently, I realized any clues would have to be culled from the work itself. I therefore retreated to the books, sleuthing through *The Confines of the Shadow*, a 300 page diary Spina kept while composing that epic, as well as three volumes of brilliant essays, and thanks to quasi-involuntary slips on Spina's part, I slowly began to assemble a narrative.

Alessandro Spina, né Basili Shafik Khouzam, was born in

Benghazi on October 8, 1927 into a family of Maronites from Aleppo. His father, a wealthy textile magnate, had left his native Syria aged 17 to make his fortune and arrived in Benghazi, the capital of Cyrenaica— then a quiet city of twenty thousand Turks and Arabs ringed by Bedouin encampments—a few weeks after Italy and the Ottoman Empire signed the Treaty of Ouchy. Ratified in October 1912, the Treaty brought 360 years of Turkish rule and 13 months of war to a close and formalized Italy's possession of Tripolitania and Cyrenaica. A latecomer to the scramble for Africa, acquiring Eritrea and Somalia in the late 1880s, barely a couple of decades after it had been cobbled out of squabbling fiefdoms, Italy had long sought to lay her hands on the *quarta sponda*, or 'fourth shore'. After all, the Libyan coast—the last remaining African territory of the Ottoman Empire, which as Baron Eversley put it, had grown used to having "provinces torn from it periodically, like leaves from an artichoke"—lay only 300 miles south of Sicily. With trouble brewing in the Balkans and sensing the sick man of Europe was on his last knees, the Italians seized their chance. Knowing they would only contend with a crippled navy and a handful of ill-equipped battalions, they delivered an ultimatum in September 1911, their soldiers disembarked in October, and by November, the Italian tricolor could be seen flying from every major city on the Libyan littoral.

Nevertheless, what was expected to be a pushover instead turned into a 20-year insurgency that was only quelled when the fascists took power in Rome and Mussolini, in a quest to solve Italy's emigration problem, dispatched one of his most ruthless generals, the hated Rodolfo Graziani (1882–1955), to bring the *quarta sponda* to heel and 'make room' for colonists. Genocide ensued: a third of Libya's population was killed, tens of thousands interned in concentration camps, a 300 kilometer barbed wire fence was erected on the Egyptian border to block rebels receiving supplies and reinforcements, and the leader of the resistance, a venerable Qur'an teacher named Omar Mukhtar (1858–1931), was hunted down and unceremoniously hanged: a chilling story elegantly depicted in *Lion of the Desert* (1981), where Oliver Reed and Anthony Quinn respectively portrayed Graziani and Mukhtar, and which was banned from Italian screens for several years.

In 1939, when Spina was 12 years old, Italy officially annexed Libya, by which time Italian settlers constituted 13% of the population and over a third of the inhabitants of Tripoli and Benghazi, the epicenters of Italian power. At the outbreak of World War Two, Spina's father dispatched his son to Italy, where he would remain until 1954. Initially leading a peripatetic existence that saw him alternate between Busto Arsizio and the spa town of Salsomaggiore, Spina and his mother eventually settled in Milan, where he became a devotee of opera: as luck would have it, the hotel where they lodged, the Marino on Piazza della Scala, was directly opposite the Teatro. While in Milan, Spina, by then fluent in Arabic, English, French and Italian, studied under Mario Marcazzan, penned a thesis on Moravia and began drafting his first stories: lush tapestries of history, fiction and autobiography featuring a cosmopolitan array of characters: Italian officers, Senussi rebels, Ottoman bureaucrats, chirpy grand dames, Maltese fishermen, aristocrats, servants and slaves. Spina nevertheless describing each caste with the same finesse, empathy and intimacy—partly thanks to his immaculate fusion of Eastern narrative quaintness and the passion for encapsulating an entire way of life that informs much 19th century European fiction, thereby distinguishing sentiment from sentimentality.

There is perhaps no better example of this balancing act than 'Il forte di Régima' / 'The Fort at Régima', one of the early stories set in the mid-1930s, where a Captain Valentini is ordered south of Benghazi to take command of a garrison stationed in an old Ottoman fortress that "recalled the castles built in Greece by knights who had joined the Fourth Crusade." Valentini is glad to leave the city and its tiresome peace-time parades behind, but as he's driven to his new posting, Valentini's mind is suddenly flooded with the names of famous Crusaders who had:

> ...conquered Constantinople, made and unmade Emperors, carved the vast Empire into fiefs, and run to and fro vainly fighting to ensure the survival of a system, which owing to its lack of roots in the country, never destined to survive.

Employing only 500 words, Spina slices across 700 years, showing the inanity of the concept of conquest, as well as the existential vacuum it inevitably leaves in its wake: "As he weltered about in his armoured vehicle, it seemed cruel to the Captain to be forced to undergo the same rigmarole after so many centuries had passed." Our technological genius may be growing, Spina implies, but so is our historical ignorance.

It's no coincidence Spina collected these sketches under the title of *Officers' Tales*. Not a single Libyan makes an appearance here and that is part of the point: it is part of Spina's pointed critique at colonial Italy's refusal to even acknowledge its native subjects. Indeed, the Italians grew so confident in their unchallenged hold over the quarta sponda over these years, that they officially annexed the province to Italy in 1939, by which time Italian settlers made up over a third of Libya's urban population and owned extensive land holdings in the interior of the country.

Those familiar with narratives of the British presence during the Raj will recognize the intimately theatrical scenes Spina sets for his readers as he chronicles an episode in Italian history that has been nearly obliterated from the country's collective memory. Time stands perfectly still in Spina's Benghazi while the ladies chatter and their husbands talk of war. The city's wide avenues are dotted with cafés where people gossip and orchestras play, yet Spina's narrators often take the reader on a tour of the surrounding area's Greek ruins—the remnants of the once-powerful city-states of the Libyan Pentapolis. Spina's tableau is vast: his stories feature haughty grande dames, industrialists, aristocrats, politicians, revolutionaries, servants, functionaries, prostitutes, dressmakers, policemen, school teachers, poets, musicians and knaves—whether in uniform or not.

This section of Spina's epic rightfully retains a militaristic feel: after all, the military was in charge in Italian Libya, and as such, many of the stories are set in the Officers' Club, where the soldiers sleep with one another's wives, plot and scheme, stage one-man shows, eat, drink, philosophize and discuss Italy's chances in the coming war, blissfully unaware that their artificial presence in that conquered land is soon to vanish entirely. Spina's Italian men-at-arms perfectly typify his concept of the 'shadow': their minds are haunted by the maddening darkness of the colonial enterprise, which still adumbrates our supposedly post-colonial times. More than a metaphor intertwining his novels, Spina's shadow can be interpreted as an allegory of how the Italian presence in Libya was both visible by dint of its brutality and yet incorporeal because it sought only to rule, never integrate. Ultimately, the shadow is also life itself: amorphous and mysterious. Mysterious because history has seen us repeatedly fail to envision what lies beyond what we can see, past the horizon of our ephemeral lives and experiences.

At the end of World War Two, Italy relinquished her claim to

Libya, which was then administered by the British until 1951, when the country became independent under King Idris I. Aged 26 and with the ink still fresh on his degree, Spina returned to Benghazi in August 1953 to help run his ageing father's factory. Although typically working twelve-hour days, he would somehow find the time to write and lock himself in his father's office, whose windows looked out onto the 14th century fondouk. Throughout his life, Spina firmly believed he'd acquired his discipline not despite being an industrialist, but because of it, in the same way Tolstoy refused to leave Yasnaya Polyana so as to stay among his people and chief source of inspiration. In his spare time, Spina would pick up the copy of Le Temps retrouvé he always kept by his side, or send letters to friends, which often featured pearls encapsulating the transformations his country was traversing:

> A young scion of the royal family – "of the highest pedigree" as Hofmannsthal might have said – the grandson of the old king who'd been deposed by the current monarch, has died in a car accident. Having come to convey his condolences, one of the King's cousins also suffered a crash on his way home to his desert encampment, an accident that took the lives of his mother, wife and son (he remains in intensive care at the hospital). I went to convey my own condolences. The Prince is very handsome, around sixty years old. He's extremely tall, his skin's a milky white and he sports a little aristocratic goatee. Eventually, the talk turned to the accident. The old man (his medieval view of the world still unmarred) remarked: "Are automobiles meant as vehicles for this world or the next?"
>
> JULY 26, 1963

During the first decade of Libyan independence, Spina completed his first collection of stories, published a novel based on his days in Milan, *Tempo e Corruzione / Time and Decay* (Garzanti, 1962), and worked on a translation of the *Storia della citta di Rame / The City of Brass* (Scheiwiller, 1963), a tale excerpted from the *One Thousand and One Nights*. However, it was only in 1964 that Spina truly hit his stride and began writing the first volumes that make up *The Confines of the Shadow*. From 1964 to 1975, arguably his most productive decade, Spina produced *Il giovane maronita / The Young Maronite* (1964–69), *Le nozze di Omar / Omar's Wedding* (1970–72), *Il visitatore notturno / The Nocturnal Visitor* (1972) and *Ingresso a Babele / Entry into Babylon*

(1973–75), which while occasionally featuring such diverse locales as Milan, Paris or Cairo, are chiefly set in Benghazi, the kilometer zero of *The Confines of the Shadow.*

The Young Maronite, the first act of the Cyrenaican saga, opens in November 1912. The new Italian Conquistadors have barricaded themselves inside Benghazi and nervously look on as the Libyans muster their strength in the desert and begin their gallant guerilla war against the usurpers. Meanwhile, Émile Chébas, a young, savvy merchant from Cairo based on Spina's father, arrives in town with a meager cargo. Émile nonetheless lands on his feet thanks to a chance encounter with Hajji Semereth Effendi, one of the city's wealthiest men and a former Ottoman grandee, who takes Émile under his wing and helps set him up, even loaning him one of his servants, Abdelkarim. Although technically the chief protagonist, it isn't until later in the book that Émile fully emerges from Semereth's, well, shadow. Spina's portrait of Semereth is immediately ensnaring:

> In Istanbul, [Semereth] had occupied several public positions that prophesied a stellar career, but after plot had been uncovered, the shadow of conspiracy had settled on him and prompted his fall. He had then withdrawn to that obscure provincial backwater and been quickly forgotten. [...] He was very tall and his face was frightening. A gunpowder charge had exploded close to him during a military campaign and he had been left forever disfigured. His hair had been reduced to a few tow-coloured clumps of locks. The wrinkles on his skull emanated a bad smell. He had an inbred seriousness and exuded an authority that made anyone who talked to him bashful and hesitant. It was like a spell that separated him from everyone else, but he was a victim of it, rather than its conscious master, as others instead assumed.

The first section deals with Semereth's unrequited love forZulfa, the youngest of his four wives, who later betrays him with Ferdinando, an orphan raised in his household. Although Semereth tries his utmost to shield the lovers from blood-baying relatives, tradition ultimately makes an honor killing inevitable: the old politician is forced to watch while Ferdinando is stabbed and Zulfa is drowned. Unbeknownst to Semereth, his family tragedy is being quietly observed by two Italian officers, who, adrift in a violently hostile land – having arrived assuming they would be welcomed as liberators—grasp onto what they can to try and make sense of their new surroundings. Of all the cast members, it's once again the officers who attempt a systemic understanding of the alien world around them, but perhaps unsurprisingly, the results are never positive. Here is Captain Romanino's take on Italy's African venture during a soirée in Milan, where he is on leave:

> Just how a language is only useful in the area in which it is spoken and is pointless outside of it, so it goes with Europe's liberal moral values, which don't extend anywhere south of the Mediterranean. As soon as one reaches the other coast, one is ordered to do the exact opposite prescribed by God's commandments: kill, steal, blaspheme...Once the Turkish garrison was defeated and a few key locations on the coast were occupied, we found a vast, obscure country stretching out before us, into which we're afraid to venture. Therefore we cloistered ourselves in the cities awaiting daylight. Instead, the night is getting deeper, darker, deadlier, and teeming with demons.

Although Spina's initial installments of *The Confines of the Shadow* attracted some notice in the mid-1970s, with several of them, including *The Young Maronite*, making the shortlists for the Strega and Campiello prizes, his presence in Libya began to grow increasingly tenuous, especially once his father's factory was nationalized in 1978. The years following Qaddafi's coup had seen the despot de-foreignize Libya, a process he began in 1970 with the expulsion of thousands of Jewish families and Italian colonists. Thus, at the age of 50, Spina witnessed the Italo-Arab-Ottoman universe he'd been born into flit away into nothingness. While this did not impair his work, it certainly impacted its publication. Case in point: although Spina had penned *The Nocturnal Visitor* over the course of a few months in early 1972, he delayed its publication until 1979 to avoid scrutiny during the turbulent early years of Qaddafi's rule when dissidents—including a number of Spina's friends—were routinely rounded up and imprisoned. In between his novels, Spina had also composed *The Fall of the Monarchy*, a history in the style of de Tocqueville that analyzes the events leading to Qaddafi's coup, which, as per Spina's wishes, will only appear posthumously. Circulated in samizdat among a select group of acquaintances, the book attracted the attentions of the security services, and when Spina left Libya for good in 1980, he was forced to smuggle the manuscript out in the French consul's briefcase. Safely removed from the reach of Qaddafi's men, Spina sojourned in Paris, and finally retired to a 17th century villa in Padergnone, in the heart of Lombard wine country, where he consecrated his buen retiro to completing *The Confines of the Shadow*, his privacy as jealously guarded as ever.

Like Joseph Roth, another inveterate chronicler of a crumbled empire, Spina had from a young age set himself to resurrecting his lost world on paper, thus ensuring its survival in our collective consciousness. While historical novels habitually focus on the rise and fall of specific castes, very few of them (Roth's *The Radetzky March* being a notable example) ever capture the confused excitement that makes the very earth those characters tread tremble with unregulated passions. As Chateaubriand once put it: "In a society which is dissolving and reforming, the struggle of two geniuses, the clash between past and future, and the mixture of old customs and new, form a transitory amalgam which does not leave a moment for boredom." It is exactly these fleeting junctures in time that infuse Spina's sophisticated prose with such an unbridled sense of adventure. Besides being the 'right' person for such a job, Spina also found himself in the right place at the right time: a Christian Arab born during the apogee of colonial power, who then consolidated his Western education with his intimate knowledge of Libyans and Middle Eastern customs and history to produce the only multi-generational epic about the European experience in North Africa.

Yet despite winning such diverse admirers as Claudio Magris, his closest confrère, Giorgio Bassani and Roberto Calasso, Spina occasionally professed surprise at the utter indifference prompted by his work, or rather his subject. Towards the end of his Diary, he recalls a run-in with the poet Vittorio Sereni at the premiere of a play in the early 1980s and being introduced to Sereni's wife: "Darling, this is Alessandro Spina, who is trying to make Italians feel guilty about their colonial crimes, all to no avail of course." Not that he hadn't been warned. When Spina had sought Moravia's advice about his project in 1960, Moravia had counselled him against it, saying no one in Italy would be interested due to their sheer nescience of the country's colonial past. Twenty-first century readers might do well to heed Solzhenitsyn's warning that "a people which no longer remembers has lost its history and its soul." Still, one must chuckle when one can: during the Libyan civil war in 2011, Spina was often approached by journalists on the hunt for sound-bites, requests that Spina invariably declined; nevertheless, I've little doubt the coincidence of the civil war being declared officially over 100 years to the day after the Italians conquered his beloved Benghazi would have made him smile.

Alessandro Spina

Two Excerpts from *The Fourth Shore*, Volume 2 of *The Confines of Shadow*, translated by André Naffis-Sahély

Military Maneuvers

"I don't know if I saw any ancient tombs on those mountains. Those tombs also belong to warriors, condottieri whose actions have been celebrated by history. They came from the East and their tombs mark their journey's exact itinerary. I retraced their steps in the opposite direction just six months ago. I had to stop at the colony's border, instead of retracing this mighty river to its source: the black stone of Arabia, the mecca of devout pilgrimages. Regretfully, I had to stop my journey far sooner than that. Yet I can't stop thinking about that long strip of tombs. On days like this, when I hear the general command shouting for war, I see yet another strip of tombs, superimposed on top of thousands of similar strips. The earth, for those who are not ignorant, like the general command, which insists on trampling on virgin lands, is a tangle of roads. Roads that have been travelled on by others before us, and which others will travel on after us."

Dismantling the camp took up the entire day. General Desiderius Occhipinti didn't seem to be in a hurry to return to the city.

Atop the camel-hump of a hill, surrounded by a wall in utter disrepair, lay an arid cemetery, where the soldiers had thrown the remains of their peeled oranges. The General hopped over the wall, followed by Captain Valentini. The General approached a tomb, which resembled a sword blade, and using his hand he carefully wiped away the dust caked around the stone. He had knelt down on one knee. The tomb was bare and porous.

"I explored up and down the entire littoral in the past few days: there are few signs indicating our presence here and they are all superficial. The arid earth, the desert, these useless shrubs: everything here contradicts our vision of the world, which, despite Fascism's guise of idealism, remains positivist at heart. There is a profound harmony between between the native's vision of their world and their natural surroundings. Our efforts, to borrow from our redundant propaganda efforts, all go to waste in the midst of nature's solemn silence. This land doesn't want us here."

The General stood up. Captain Valentini helped him up with his arm. The youthful Lieutenant Rossi was waiting for them at the bottom of the cemetery.

"What's your opinion on this, Captain? Will the English be the ones who turf us out of this colony, or will be it the natural violence of this very land that chases us away? Last Saturday's sand storm, just before the maneuvers began, was truly frightening. One day I think we'll disappear in exactly the same manner: as though the earth had swallowed us up, or as though the winds had hurled us into the ocean. The colony is an artificial organism, and we are destined to die."

A Solitary Duel

"Literature is reality's dress uniform," Major Morelli's wife said, slipping her foot into a purple velvet shoe.

Reserved and aloof, as though on display in the shop windows, the ladies were selecting their footwear for the New Year's Eve Ball in Treni's cobbler store. Mrs Occhipinti had a golden sandal in her hand.

The cobbler, a ridiculous and repugnant-looking little beast, was sat at Mrs Borletti's feet. He always struck a gracious pose, light as a pixie. These movements were his exaggerated way of recognizing how ridiculous he looked. There was something pathetic and heartrending in all that ostentatiousness. The ladies were nevertheless drawn to it, as they slipped their feet into the shoe held by his cupped hands with sensual repugnance.

Mrs Borletti laughed. "There's something death-like and funereal about literature...," she said, somewhat embarrassedly. "Truth be told," she added, lifting her index finger, "the spirit freezes life in time. My dear," she exclaimed, leaning her upper body forward, "aren't you feeling well?"

"I'm fine, I'm fine," Mrs Occhipinti calmly replied, raising her hand. She hated compassion. She had spent two months in the hospital; she had been released against her doctors' wishes so she could celebrate Christmas and new year's eve with her husband, the General of the Army Corps, Desiderius Occhipinti.

The hospital's head physician had stammered when he'd told the General: "I refuse any and all responsibility..." Occhipinti had shot him a cold stare. Then he had given his arm to his wife, and as though he could barely notice the pitiful effort it took her to walk, he had left alongside her. The General's orderly, standing to attention out on the street, while holding the car door open, was filled with terror at the sight of that woman as she walked along in tiny, mechanical jerks.

"Are you sure you don't need anything, darling? Maybe you're tired?"

Mrs Occhipinti thrust her leg forward, as though kicking away her friend's pitiful voice, or wanting to prove her strength. The sandal flew off her foot and landed in a corner.

Lieutenant Mazzei appeared in the shop window's frame, looking as though wanting to smash it and step inside.

A couple of days later, during the Christmas dinner held at the Prefect's house, the guests paid particular attention to her. Mrs Occhipinti remained impassive and her sentences were cold and curt.

The Prefect's wife had welcomed Mrs Occhipinti with the most unrestrained and intense pity imaginable – as though in a romantic novel, the highlight of the day. Yet she had been rudely refused. Mrs Occhipinti was a dark guest: aggressive and hard-edged, she had not come to put her agony on display, but rather her strength. The Prefect's wife was convinced that Mrs Occhipinti's illness was merely her just punishment for her sins. Thus, her strength – a blatant display of pride and presumptiousness – struck the Prefect's wife as completely sacrilegious. *Our house has been profaned,* she thought to herself, alarmed.

General Occhipinti hadn't kept track of his wife's mistakes. He refused to connect her mistakes to her illness, or to think of her condition as a form of punishment, like the Prefect's wife did. In the same manner, he also allowed her to suffer while he sat next to her, silent. Only his behavior had been normal when he'd accompanied his wife out of the hospital, or taken her to the Prefect's house for dinner, free of all bother and orotundity: it appeared as though he knew nothing of the devils looking to waylay his wife on her path.

The Prefect, who perceived the General as enigmatic, had once asked him why he'd opted for a career in the military. "Because it's the only way of life that is scientifically precise."

He abhorred confiding in people, as though doing so would violate a rule.

The halls of the Officers' Club were brightly lit and empty. They would remain open until four in the morning.

The Cathedral was crowded with people. The Bishop had already made his entrance, having been preceded by his priests. Having descended from his palace and crossed the square, the Bishop had entered through the large gates. All in black, and lined up in serried ranks, the nuns sang choir.

The officers were wearing their dress uniforms.

"His Majesty doesn't speak," Captain Sorrentino said. "We would just need a nod of his head to sweep Fascism away like dust." He took in the club's hall, crossing it in great strides. He was irritated and restless. "Well, what's stopping him?"

"He would certainly prefer a more cautious kind of Fascism," Colonel Verri said, having a penchant for indulging the Captain's temperament, "and an even falser and more hypocritical one too while we're at it. In other words," he added with a smile, "one that is both more civic and cynical. But maybe he's worried that any attempt to perfect it will ultimately weaken it, and make it incapable of withstanding an opponent's blows."

"Why doesn't the army take the initiative? If the King's isn't able to lead us, he will at least follow us."

"Alas, my dear friend, don't fill your head with too many delusions. Nobody's going to make a move. We have compromised ourselves too much already. The declaration of war is like a messenger who can no longer be stopped. We'll fight that war, for better or worse! Then, one after the other, the king and his subjects, the army and the fascist dissidents will start to make their move. Or maybe it will happen the other way around. Meaning everyone will show up late! By that time, we'll probably be able to prove that we had never wanted the war in the first place."

"But why are we just accepting all of this? Why?" The Captain's irritation was sharply in relief, and the Colonel observed him indulgently. He was a man at his peak who was hesitant to squander his energies in a time of mediocrity. This contradiction held the key to his destiny.

Captain Sorrentino stopped in the middle of the hall. "Our only hope then is that Mussolini comes back to his senses and stops before he falls over the precipice and just sends us home."

The Colonel smiled. "Opinions!" he said cheerfully, "Because it might turn out to be the worst solution, prolonging slavery for an indeterminate amount of time. Our lives grow ever more inward and empty. If he pulls back from this abyss, the Duce might assume greater powers for himself. We'll owe him for that too, for defending us from Fascism's fatal outcome."

"So we don't have a choice!" the Captain exclaimed in an excessively cheerful manner.

"You're wrong there," the Colonel retorted, "if we manage to save our skins, then we'll have saved everything. There are always plausible reasons for coming to terms with one's past. If in the end we don't come to war, we'll keep living as are now forever: the king, his subjects, the army and the fascist dissidents. There's an empty void inside me and I don't know how I'll ever fill it. I don't expect anything out of war. But if I have to survive it, I don't want the price to be an apology! If they are willing to forgive my sins, then I won't bother them with my explanations and justifications. Maybe I just don't love life enough: trials and explanations strike me as utterly ridiculous."

"This Christmas mass has been going on for ages," Captain Sorrentino said, returning to his seat. He didn't feel like singing hymns anymore.

"The Christmas mass and the military review to mark the anniversary of the Charter, the ball in the Governor's palace and the great maneuvers: without these spectacles, life here would become unbearable. Mussolini keeps us entertained as though we were courtesans."

"Go on, I said, I don't need anything."

The voice hailed from beyond the tomb. Colonel Verri and Captain Sorrentino jumped to their feet. They were barely able to nod their heads to the General of the Army Corps Desiderius Occhipinti, who was on his way out. His wife lay seated in a corner of the sitting room. The dinner at the Prefect's house had been a challenging trial. The tension caused by the people around her was consuming her.

Colonel Verri crossed the sitting room. He bowed. Captain Sorrentino stood next to him, lingering impassively like a guard. The General's wife observed them without moving. She then extended her arm so that the Colonel could hold it devotedly in his to plant a kiss on it.

The General's wife hadn't left the hospital in order to be pitied, as some of the Prefect's wife's guests suspected, but merely to be able to watch and listen, so that life could start flowing freely before her eyes once again, instead of going around in circles at the hospital.

The Colonel took a seat next to the General's wife. Counsel and Strength, here they were, the two last loyal men: the General's wife eyed one, then the other, as though probing them.

The sitting room's emptiness was as heavy as sleep. The General's wife felt like giving in to it. The compassionate attention the Prefect's guests had paid her had nevertheless irritated her and thus reawakened her strength. The chatter at the Officers' Club was a spider-web, and it wasn't strong enough to keep her for long.

She suddenly dropped her neck, like a swaying drunk. The Colonel smiled kindly at her and interpreting that nod as a sign, he turned to his friend and said:

"To tell the truth, my dear Captain, we are unable to overcome the *petty religious root of our problem*. From a social point of view, it's a mistake. Few among us are in fact citizens. The army is a mystical body. Hierarchy aside, the exceptional importance we give to form and following the rules imply faith, as well as a *common faith*, which we nonetheless lack."

The General's wife's eyes grew wide. She had grasped the last sentence, like an image caught immediately after waking up, and she had mulled on it without managing to penetrate its meaning. She felt such an intense and unbearable solitude that a cry almost escaped her lips. She pressed a handkerchief against her mouth. Silence! Silence!

The Captain looked at her admiringly.

"Among the most passionate of us, opposites become interchangeable," the Colonel said, "dread and restlessness for war, execration and indifference towards fascism, the anxiety for a renaissance and the certainty of not being up to its task. Even if *good* manages to triumph, meaning that the righteous win (or at least the ones closest to righteousness) can such an outcome change destiny and allow me to reconcile myself to life? I am dutiful when it comes to my work, just like others are. But it's nothing but pride – or just an easy solution. In this confused war, many of us will serve with great dignity, and perhaps even with heroism when the occasion calls for it. But what will all this praiseworthy behavior really mean? Selfishness is foreign to a religious soul. I shall calmly trust what my superior officers tell me. Yet what others will go looking for when we begin to move towards the enemy, that I don't know. But look they will."

The sitting room was deserted. The stuccoes on the ceiling and walls had a sepulchral magnificence to them. All in all, the room's decoration was of a funereal character, and exaggeratedly consoling.

"What will humanity's fate be, then?" The Captain asked. He nevertheless lacked the earlier spring in his step. The appearance of the General's wife had left him distracted. Was all that agony – and the General's wife clutched her willpower as though it were a sword – noble or sacrilegious? What sense was there to all that effort?

"War is a game to change the way the world is ordered," the Colonel insisted, "but neither camp is capable of reconquering my faith in life. The impulse to commit suicide springs from an inability to hold a dialogue with the events of the world around us. *Self-awareness* is a prison into which we throw ourselves while waiting (or looking) for a purpose. This is as far as our education allows us to go. Or allows us to go."

"What fruitless effort!" Captain Sorrentino angrily exclaimed, coming to a stop smack in the middle of the room. The General's wife was motionless. The Captain looked at that silvery face: he watched it float against the wall like the moon in a limpid sky. "We should instead seek to reach a positive solution, one azure enough to spread around the entire world."

The General's wife smiled with joy. That word – azure – had stirred her.

The Captain crossed the room with only a few steps. "I'm going to tell you a story," he announced.

"This," he said, laying the palm of his hand on the table in front of him, "is the Fortress." He showed her. "It's an orderly and isolated complex." he explained. The General's wife listened attentively. His words seemed clear enough to her. That clarity already heralded the azure that had been mentioned.

The Captain didn't bandy on about what that Order might be, it wasn't necessary. The story would have the brevity of dreams, and share their burning immediacy.

"Against the Fortress, is the Hero." The Captain took two paces to his right, and looking inexplicably youthful, he bowed before his public. Then, standing erect, he headed towards the little table.

"A conflict is born when a hero can no longer endure their isolation, and the repugnance her feels for the intangibility of Order. Owing to its isolation and immobility, the Fortress stands outside of time and experience."

The Captain walked around the table three times, while keeping his eyes fixed on it. With each turn, he bent his knees a little further.

Then suddenly he stood up to his full height and turned on his heels.

"The young man escapes!" and he took a couple of steps away, approaching his spectators and thus subtracting himself from their gaze. The table had been left behind the middle of the room.

"The people of the Fortress refuse to take note of this flight, and feign ignorance: but time and experience seep through and infiltrate the gaps left by the Hero's escape."

"That departure was a wound." The Colonel burst out.

The General's wife was following the story very attentively.

"But the young man," the Captain resumed, stepping back on the scene as though having just returned from a trip around the world and had wound up at the starting point again, "comes back and stays. The opening created by his departure is plugged up by his return. The Fortress welcomes the young man as though it had just emerged from an illness, or freed itself from the germs of an infection, and recovers its initial harmony. Life in the Fortress carries on, in a repetitive circular motion, including: the addition of another young man."

The image of the circle pleased the General's wife. The present was only the darkest hour of the night. But azure was a path. She smiled cheerfully once again. Growing calmer, she nodded: the Captain was free to continue.

Sorrentino launched into it again, yet this time in a threatening tone, and laying his palm on the table again, he said: "The Fortress has been besieged."

At which point he accosted the spectators to explain. "This time it has nothing to do with germs of an infection, or an illness of the organism, or rather of one of its cells (the Hero): it's an external force."

With soldier-like, booming steps, the Captain advanced towards the Fortress. Once he'd arrived in front of the table, he suddenly turned around. His features were tense. "The young man defends the Fortress with incredible doggedness."

The tension on his features left no doubt as to the young man's determination.

Then, loosening his arms, which had previously lain still, he added: "All one needs to notice in this edifying turn is the young man's exaggerated effort, which is vaguely ambiguous, and his loving violence when faced with the enemy; it is so different from the cold, calculating and impersonal determination of the others."

The Captain repeated the same movement many times over: he would spin around halfway and then stop and show only his face. Another half turn and another stop. Both spins were so similar that in the end, partly owing to the speed of his movements, they came to identify with one another.

"The external force, the only external force, appears to coincide with death: and as it happens the young man is killed. His heroic behavior shares the same enthusiasm as the moment of escape. When that journey has failed, especially as an experience meant to renew the Order of things, death appears as the only force, or reality – and place – that is foreign to the Fortress. From the enthusiasm of the journey, and optimism, to the pessimistic heroism of the final battle, polluted by romantic leaps and moody suicides."

"Very good," the Colonel said, smiling indulgently, "that's exactly what I meant to say: you never know what the Hero is looking for when he moves towards the enemy."

The General's wife looked at the Captain with her icy eyes, she could barely even move them anymore, like a puppet whose strings have all snapped. She nevertheless kept her head straight and her eyelids open.

Once they had left the Cathedral, the officers poured into the club. The ballroom was still empty, and people milled around in the large entrance hall.

The young lieutenant Mazzei crossed the ballroom. For a moment further, he lingered like a lost messenger in a crowd. Behaving as one who reaches the end of a road, he went to stand before the General's wife and there came to a stop.

After a dramatic silence, he directed his eyes towards hers, which diverged.

The eye staring straight ahead allowed her to see what she was about to lose forever, youth, beauty and life; while the other eye remained enigmatic. She had used up all her strength on the eye looking straight ahead without bringing the other eye in line with it. She made a supreme effort: to keep them firmly fixed in the direction of Lieutenant Mazzei's eyes, maybe this was the solution to all enigmas.

The public flowed towards the ballroom, where a banquet had been laid out.

Now that he had been left alone in the oblong hall adjacent to the main ballroom, Captain Sorrentino crossed it in a pacey manner. Surly and incredibly highly-strung, he had finally found an outlet in the parody of that tragedy.

"I am convinced that Fascism is unequal to tragedy! And it is frightening, frightening! Not only is nobody making a move here, but even the Great Powers aren't moving."

"We do not have a destiny," he added, disdainfully.

"What a great bargain, eh?" the Colonel muttered.

"Without Nazism, Fascism wouldn't be able to bring us closer to tragedy. It's nothing but a minor, mediocre scandal. Without the Nazis, we'll be forced to side with the powers of democracy against the Soviets. And if the Nazis are defeated, the fascist remnants will be incorporated by the democratic powers in their struggle against communism. Nazism is the barrier holding back the tide of that disgrace. We the oppressed will never rebel against the regime, neither will the latter ever exceed the colonial confines of its misdeeds and boldness, nor will our friends make war upon us, since it would be seen as unforgivably impatient to waste any soldiers' lives in our national comedy, which is so provincial – Hitler will declare war and it will be fought against him. That is a scandal, but fascism isn't. At least it isn't considered a scandal by our collective conscience, which is so accommodating, nor is it deemed so by those well-disposed towards the compromise made by the democratic powers. Hitler has overstepped, and the fire has been lit. Our neighbor's house is about to go up in flames, and we'll wind up burned alongside him. Deceived by the nature of that fire, we drew close to it in order to conveniently warm ourselves up, but by the time we'll want to leave it'll be too late. In other words, we'll suffer the same fate as that of a stupid servant who is in thrall to a diabolical master. Only when our entire house has gone up in flames will we be able to rediscover ourselves. Even the king, who binds us all together via that solemn oath of loyalty, will manage to do this."

General Occhipinti appeared on the scene. "Darling, do you want to come into the next room? A service is being held by the Christmas tree."

He offered her his arm. The General's wife concentrated all her energies on that spot. Her hands stirred on the armrests, and blood slowly flowed through her whole body again. She looked like a snake exerting itself. Yet she stood up, and took her husband's arm. She crossed the sitting room and entered the ballroom.

A few chairs had been positioned right in front of the orchestra. In the middle lay a gigantic Christmas tree. Slivers of silver foil were hanging from its branches. The General's wife sat down. She was alert and felt that she was being watched, just like at the Prefect's house. The presence of people gave her strength – and gnawed at her. She composed her features into a smile.

In order to make the Christmas tree stand out even further, the ballroom's lighting had been arranged in an unusual manner. Almost all of the available light shone on the tree and the few guests of honor. The other guests were nothing more than an iridescent dust cloud of jewels and decorations. The stuccoes appeared to be hanging like festoons off the azure strip running alongside all the walls. The orchestra, which was only composed of string instruments, played a slow, melancholic melody, yet did so discreetly in order not to disturb the mysterious, nocturnal harmony. There was a strong visual character to the service, while the music was instead merely secondary, complementary. Yet the General's wife nevertheless listened to it attentively.

A male voice rang out clear, filling the room and dominating the sweet sounds of the string instruments. The General's wife felt she was hanging by that thread. There was no doubt that this service aimed to bring her in the direction of that divergent eye, to the blue spot that the latter was pointing out. Her composed smile dissolved into cheerfulness. "Aren't you feeling well, darling?" The General asked, bending down towards her.

> "......................*sparget sonum*
>
> ....
>
> ....*ante thronum*
>
> ....*et natura.*"[1]

The General's wife was hanging by the thread of that hymn.

To the right, the young officers were lined up like priests. The General's wife gaze examined them one after the other. It seemed to her as though she was moving, carried along on a stretcher towards the destination which her sight had denied her, but which her ears had already found. The General, who was now sat beside her, waited for an answer. The General's wife replied with a nod. She feared being distracted, and the service required all her powers of concentration. She kept her arms along the chair's armrests, and followed the slow, musical rhythm of the priests' footsteps. She looked to the left, at the officers and the ladies. The dress uniforms and all that impeccable grooming charged the scene with tension. The General's wife straightened her bust. She dominated the scene with her head.

The General's wife was hanging by the thread of the singer's voice. She barely caught a few words. Maybe she distorted them or misinterpreted them, since she alone heard other words being sung. All of a sudden, making a convulsive gesture, she recognized that hymn, which they were trying to pass off as a sweet, innocent Christmas song.

> "*Judex ergo cum sedebit*
>
> *Quidquid latet apparebit...*"

The procession came to a sudden stop, the line of young priests broke up, while the officers and ladies on the right took a step back,

---

[1] Excerpts from the Latin Christian hymn, *Dies Irae*, or Day of Wrath.

frightened.

The singer took a single step forward on the stage and the General's wife was filled with terror when she recognized Lieutenant Mazzei's divergent eyes. She kept her lids forcefully open. There could no longer be any doubts: that young man was her death.

"Do you want to leave, darling?"

Here was the warrior who had come from afar, the Guest calling out for her, for whom "the use of darling and excuses" were worth nothing at all. The doors swung open, and the Fortress's inhabitants held their breath.

Victory belonged to the other. The fatal duel – the General's wife nursed no doubts as to the final outcome – thus resolved itself into an attitude problem. When it came to duels between knights, reason and outcome had no bearing, but one's attitude, which was equated to one's honor, did have bearing. One could move against the enemy with the kind of loving leap that Captain Sorrentino had described. Or one could oppose the cold light of self-awareness, and push the limits of life to the extreme.

The azure point, the supernatural, is only death – a door which opens only to reveal nothing, a loss which doesn't match up with any purchases. How does one enter through that door?

A lover's tremor, a prisoner's dignity...

A warrior clutching a sword stands by the door.

The General's wife straightened her bust, kept her head level and her eyelids open. The procession of priests reassembled itself. Then it began to move.

The lifeless body of the General's wife was carried out. The General dismissed those friends who had offered to accompany him.

Colonel Verri and Captain Sorrentino were sat on the last empty chairs. "Mazzei disappeared," the Captain said. The Colonel smiled. "I can't think of anything more irritating than this music,", the Captain remarked, irked. "I was in the other room when Mazzei started to sing. He took my breath away, and now we're listening to this garbage again!"

"Oh yes," the Colonel replied, "but did you notice the damage those musical notes inflicted?... they cost The General's wife her life!"

"So let's re-immerse ourselves in this garbage then," the Captain said, scanning his surroundings. "At least it won't cost anyone their life."

Vexed, the Captain stood up and left.

The Confines of the Shadow is published in the US by Arcade (Vol. 1 *The Colonial Conquest*, Vol. 2 *The Fourth Shore*) and in the UK by DARF (Vol. 1 *The Confines of the Shadow*, Vol. 2 *Colonial Tales*).

Lisa Anderson

A Pool of Water: Perspectives on the Libyan Revolution

Books reviewed (in chronological order):

Hisham Matar, *The Return: Fathers, Sons and the Land in Between*, New York, Random House, 2016

Peter Cole and Brian McQuinn, eds., *The Libyan Revolution and Its Aftermath*, New York: Oxford University Press, 2015

Christopher Chivvis, *Toppling Qaddafi: Libya and the Limits of Liberal Intervention*, New York: Cambridge University Press, 2014

Ethan Chorin, *Exit the Colonel: The Hidden History of the Libyan Revolution*, New York: Public Affairs, 2012

Maximilian Forte, *Slouching Towards Sirte: NATO's War on Libya and Africa*, Montreal: Baraka Books, 2012

Lindsey Hilsum, *Sandstorm: Libya in the Time of Revolution*, New York: The Penguin Press, 2012

Alison Pargeter, *Libya: The Rise and Fall of Qaddafi*, New Haven: Yale University Press, 2012

THE UPRISING THAT BROUGHT DOWN THE REGIME of Muammar Qaddafi in Libya in 2011 was a conflagration that touched every Libyan, both within the country and beyond, and transfixed observers throughout the world. As upheavals convulsed neighboring Tunisia and Egypt, the drama, daring and difficulty of the rebellion in Libya provoked the Arab League and the United Nations to acquiesce in a NATO-led military intervention; it briefly seemed that the whole world cared about the future of Libya. The capture and execution of Qaddafi at the end of October 2011, after ten months of brutal battle, was both a remarkable victory and, as it turned out, an enormous challenge. The rebuilding of Libya was not a task the rest of the world cared to take on nor a project for which Libyans themselves were well-prepared.

Like a pool of water, Libya seems to reflect the images of those who peer into it as often as it reveals its own depths. This review of books published in the aftermath of the uprising illustrates the puzzling complexity of this small country.[1] The debates about the country's role in the world, the character of its leaders, the meaning of its history and the prospects for its future are all on display. All these books were published in English within five years of the revolution;[2] all but one of them are by Europeans or Americans—journalists, government officials, and academics—the exception is a memoir by a British-Libyan novelist, Hisham Matar. As he remarks:

> All the books on the modern history of the country could fit neatly on a couple of shelves...A Libyan hoping to glimpse something of that past must, like an intruder at a private party, enter such books in the full knowledge that most of them were not written by or for [them], and, therefore, at heart, they are accounts concerning the lives of others, their adventures and misadventures in Libya, as though one's country is but an opportunity for foreigners

---

[1]   As is always the case in works on Libya, the authors of these works follow widely differing conventions in transliterating names of people and places. Although it has meant some inconsistency in this essay, I have reproduced each authors' usage without comment or correction, confident that readers will be able to determine who and what is being discussed. The numbers that follow direct quotations refer the reader to the pages of the relevant volume.

[2]   Frederic Wehrey's *The Burning Shores: Inside the Battle for the New Libya* (London: Farrar, Straus and Giroux, 2018) was published seven years after the demise of the Qaddafi regime and therefore falls outside the scope of this review. It bears mentioning, however, for it may illustrate the value of a little historical perspective; it is easily the best single volume available on Libyan politics today, exhibiting not only extensive knowledge but unusual sympathy with the many Libyans who struggle to secure peace and prosperity at home.

to exorcize their demons and live out their ambitions.[3]

The books examined here bear out Matar's observation: they are as often about the hopes and dreams of foreigners as they are about Libya itself, reflecting all too well the country's struggle to define its place in the world and to write its own history.

International influences: Libya in the world

A useful starting point in examining how the literature about the Libyan uprising portrays the country is to look at the geopolitical context. After all, Libya had been a "pariah state" for decades when the rebellion broke out, only relatively recently rehabilitated, and still a mystery to many outside the country. As Chorin tells us in his gossipy, well-informed and often affectionate account, he volunteered to serve as the commercial/economic officer at the newly opened US Liaison Office in Tripoli in 2004-6 because "there were few places in the region...that could be said to be so exotic."[4]

Two of these books see Libya almost entirely as a puzzle piece, or perhaps better, as one of the billiard balls of classic realist international relations theory. The fact that the authors know little about the country is no impediment to their arguments since they are concerned with the geopolitics of international support for the revolt.

Christopher Chivvis, a political scientist at the RAND Corporation who was, as he puts it "working in the Pentagon at the time," provides a clear, dispassionate, technocratic account of the decision-making that lead to the NATO intervention. He argues that

> the need to design cost-effective solutions to crises such as the one that occurred in Libya in March 2011 will be with us for many years. The study of what was and was not accomplished in Libya gives insight into both the limits and the potential for liberal intervention—the use of force to protect the basic liberal values of human

---

[3]   Hisham Matar, *The Return: Fathers, Sons and the Land in Between*, 131–32.

[4]   Chorin, *Exit The Colonel: The Hidden History of the Libyan Revolution*, 3.

rights, the rule of law, and constitutional government.[5]

Chivvis seems oblivious to the fact that virtually none of those "liberal values" existed in Libya to be protected, either before or after the NATO intervention, and he spends relatively little time on Libya as such—the controversies he recounts are all in Washington. He does acknowledge that "the intervention will certainly look different if Libya collapses back into a lengthy civil war [or] another dictator emerges from the fray"[6] but this simply begs the question of whether those who planned and executed the intervention should have considered the domestic political scene more carefully.

In fact, Chivvis documents astonishing ignorance about Libya in Washington, describing what he calls "basic uncertainty" and outlining "a number of conceivable outcomes" that any informed Libya watcher would have deemed outlandish: "If the country ended up divided between a liberated east and Qaddafi ruled west postconflict planning would only be necessary in the east. If there was a negotiated settlement in which Qaddafi stepped down but the regime stayed in power, it was unclear how reconstruction would proceed." And even when more plausible scenarios were considered, the uppermost concern seems not to have been their desirability but the budget: "There was also...growing concern that Qaddafi might conduct a scorched earth campaign that could make postwar resource requirements skyrocket."[7]

Chivvis acknowledges mission creep: the ostensible rationale of the NATO intervention—the new United Nations doctrine known as "Responsibility to Protect"—quickly became regime change. But he says, "there is no evidence for claims that the United States and its allies duped other members of the Security Council into voting for a limited intervention when they fully intended to topple Qaddafi from the outset..."[8] Perhaps not, but US President Barack Obama declared that Qaddafi had "lost the legitimacy to rule and needs to do what it

---

[5] Chivvis, *Toppling Qaddafi*, xv.

[6] Chivvis, *Toppling Qaddafi*, 14.

[7] Chivvis, *Toppling Qaddafi*, 144–45.

[8] Chivvis, *Toppling Qaddafi*, 179.

right for the country by leaving now."[9] This sounds a lot like a call for regime change.

Chivvis' declaration that the operation "has rightly been hailed as a success" also obscures the fact that its objectives were ambiguous and changeable. "In seven months of operations," he says, "the intervening powers maintained an arms embargo, facilitated humanitarian relief, created and sustained a no-fly zone, and helped protect Libya's civilian population from depredation at the hands of Qaddafi's forces."[10] Yet that is not entirely true, however, since arms poured into the country throughout the fighting. As for "longer-term political objectives," he tells us that it will be "many years" before we know if they were achieved. No doubt that is true, since no-one seems to know what they were.

Maxmilian Forte, a professor of anthropology at Concordia University, is sure he knows what the objectives of NATO intervention were and he rehearses his argument eloquently, if ultimately unpersuasively, in *Slouching Towards Sirte: NATO's war on Libya and Africa*. Forte summarizes his position succinctly: the West is driven by neo-imperialism and "NATO's campaign represents the continued militarization of Western and especially U.S, foreign policy and the rise of the new 'military humanism.'"[11] This argument is plausible; after all, the notion that some governments have the "responsibility to protect" the citizens of another country against their own rulers has been a convenient rationale for imperialists for centuries. Recall that, when they invaded the Libyan territories in 1911, the Italians announced that they had come "not to subdue and enslave the populations of Tripolitania, Cyrenaica and other countries of the interior, now under bondage to the Turks, but to restore them their rights, punish the despots, make them free and in control of themselves, and to protect them against those very despots..."[12] The ease with which the NATO

---

[9] Chivvis, *Toppling Qaddafi*, 117.

[10] Cited in Forte, *Slouching Towards Sirte: NATO's War on Libya and Africa*, 174.

[11] Forte, *Slouching Towards Sirte*, 9.

[12] Quoted in Eileen Ryan, *Religion as Resistance: Negotiating Authority in Italian Libya, 1911-1931* (Oxford: Oxford University Press, 2018).

mission slid from "protection of civilians" to "regime change" gives ample reason for skepticism about such humanitarian intervention.

Forte begins to lose this reader, however, when he further argues that the purpose of this militarization was to "disrupt an emerging pattern of independence and a network of collaboration within Africa that would facilitate increased African self-reliance."[13] Certainly, there were many non-Libyans, in Africa and elsewhere, who appreciated Qaddafi's willingness to flout Western norms and rules. Nelson Mandela, for example, was deeply appreciative of Libyan support for the ANC during apartheid, as were many other less well-known or, perhaps, less successful anti-imperialist and revolutionary movements, from the IRA to the PLO. Yet a criticism of the NATO intervention, even one that sees it as an integral part of a vast American neo-imperial strategy in Africa, need not be quite as uncritical and forgiving of the Qaddafi regime as Forte is.

Qaddafi deployed Libya's vast oil wealth to buy friends and allies throughout Africa quite instrumentally and cynically. This was not about "African self-reliance"—Nelson Mandela's longstanding loyalty to Qaddafi notwithstanding—so much as sowing disorder across the continent. As the British journalist Lindsey Hilsum recounts in *Sandstorm*, her fast-paced and even-handed account of the uprising, students came from all over the world to Qaddafi's World Center for Resistance against Imperialism, Zionism, Racism, Reaction and Fascism. "But the list of African alumni is striking for the chaos they brought to their home countries: Charles Taylor, who turned Liberia into a killing ground...Foday Sankoh, whose forces in Sierra Leone were notorious for chopping off people's arms and legs; Laurent Kabila, who ousted Mobutu Sese Seko in Zaire and presided over an equally brutal regime..."[14]

Forte focuses his defense of Qaddafi's regime in a clever and provocative focus on Sirte, both as Qaddafi's favored city within Libya and as his choice for the capital of the "United States of Africa" he hoped to build. Few observers would give Sirte the prominence in Libyan, much less African, history as Forte does, and it provides a

---

[13] Forte, *Slouching Towards Sirte*, 137.

[14] Forte, *Slouching Towards Sirte*, 154.

useful lens through which to examine the support for the Qaddafi regime. But in portraying Libya under Qaddafi as "prosperous, independent and defiant,"[15] Forte understates the damage the regime wrought both within Libya and beyond its borders. Moreover, in using Libya as a case study of Western neo-imperialism in Africa, he misses the role of other international actors. The history of the involvement of Turkey and Qatar, Egypt and the UAE, for example, whose support of rival factions among the revolutionaries remained a serious hindrance to reconciliation many years after the Qaddafi regime had collapsed, is yet to be written but should not be forgotten.

If the nature of international support for the Libya uprising is still contested, the same is even more true of the domestic scene within Libya. Indeed, the several "current history" accounts of the Libyan revolution under review here provide striking illustration of the use of history itself as both a weapon and a shield, and most of the foreign analysts seem to be unaware of (or perhaps unconcerned by) the political biases embedded in the interpretations of Libyan history they recite.

The Recent Past: Divisions within the Old Regime

Let us start with what should be a simple question; how did the uprising start? Obviously, we know that in a context of upheaval in neighboring Tunisia and Egypt, the arrest of human rights lawyer Fathi Terbil sparked a demonstration in Benghazi on 15 February by around 200 relatives of prisoners killed by Libyan security forces in a well-documented massacre in Abu Salim Prison in 1996. A 'Day of Rage' followed on February 17, during which there were protests across the country. On February 20, Saif al-Islam al-Qaddafi, "the reformist son, negotiator, compromiser and his father's foil" gave an incendiary speech in which he "had gone, apparently overnight, from being the compensator for his father's lunacy to a replica of it."[16] Soon thereafter the Minister of Justice resigned from the government, to be followed by the Interior Minister, the chief prosecutor, and numerous

---

[15] Forte, *Slouching Towards Sirte*, 10.

[16] Chorin, *Exit the Colonel: The Hidden History of the Libyan Revolution*, 197.

ambassadors. By February 27, the formation of a National Transition Council was announced in Benghazi to act as the "political face of the revolution." The uprising was underway.

As Chorin reminds us, many, if not most, of the prominent figures in the early days of the uprising had worked within the system, as lawyers, judges, diplomats; they were members of what might be called the reform wing of the Qaddafi regime. He thus dates the beginning of the end of the Qaddafi regime to the failure of both the regime and the US to take advantage of the 2003 deal that ended decades of Libyan isolation. It could have "afforded an opportunity for both sides, Libya and the West, to make a break with the past, to refashion the relationship into something more mature and potentially sustainable."[17] He asks "a key question...whether the Libyan youth, the raw material of the revolution, could have sustained this uprising, without an added element, a cadre that could coordinate actions in the wake of the 'Day of Rage' and resulting street battles, while articulating the rudiments of a plan...." And his answer is unequivocal:

> Qaddafi's reformists, and the concentric circles of individuals who either found reformist dialogue profitable or believed it was possible, provided this critical ingredient. Ironically, then, many people who were "of the regime" and are currently criticized for the association, may have been a necessary transitional ingredient. Would the US have responded to the pleas for help from individuals about who they knew absolutely nothing?[18]

Whether he knows it or not, Chorin echoes a longstanding hypothesis in political science that the breakdown of an authoritarian regime begins with cracks in the regime itself. "Hard-liners" and "soft-liners" appear and the soft-liners make tacit or explicit alliances with members of the opposition—what Chorin describes in the Libyan context as "the Islamist opposition, commercial activists and dissident groups."[19] In peaceful transitions, the reassurance that members of the regime

---

[17] Chorin, *Exit the Colonel*, 306.

[18] Chorin, *Exit the Colonel*, 268.

[19] Chorin, *Exit the Colonel*, 270.

itself will be afforded a role in a successor government or at least a safe exit is often part of an explicit political pact; in revolutionary transitions, history suggests that the "liberals" in both the regime and the opposition are more likely to be cast aside during a Jacobin Reign of Terror.[20]

Hilsum is less sanguine than Chorin about the potential of the post-sanctions regime in Libya, arguing, "while Libya was emerging from isolation, the regime was becoming less of a dictatorship and more of a mafia.... Qaddafi's cousins and in-laws has always been appointed to senior positions, but now it was the children's turn."[21] In fact, they are probably both right: like Gamal Mubarak in Egypt, Saif al-Islam wanted to inherit a regime that reflected the imperatives of power in the twenty-first century and that required reform. The Libyan regime's increasing reliance on kin went hand-in-hand with a simultaneous systematic outreach to regime skeptics and even opponents in the years between 2003 and 2010.

That Saif's interest in reform was instrumental should probably have been no surprise but when Saif gave his uncompromising speech on February 20, 2011 the shock and disappointment was widespread. Chorin, Hilsum, and Alison Pargeter, a research analyst and consultant based in London, whose *Libya: The Rise and Fall of Qaddafi* is an often casual and even flippant account of Libyan history and politics, all spend pages parsing Saif's motives. They, like many of the Libyans who worked with him, wonder whether the Saif they saw in that speech was a sincere reformer whose father and brothers had intimidated him into abandoning his liberal convictions or an unprincipled prince who had professed liberal convictions merely to win international and elite support for his ambitions. Certainly the process of negotiation around resolution of the Lockerbie affair and the relinquishing of all capabilities to manufacture or deploy weapons of mass destruction (WMD), both of which Saif championed, suggest more expediency than sincerity, a willingness to do—and pay—anything to lift sanctions that were damaging the family patrimony. As Hisham Matar puts it in his

---

[20] The first is exemplified by the transitions in Southern Europe and Latin America in the 1970s and 1980s; the second by the historic revolutions—France, Russia, China and, most recently, Iran—in which the radical ideologues eventually turned on their moderate, liberal or nationalists, allies.

[21] Hilsum, *Sandstorm*, 168–69.

Anderson

memoir of his search for his father, a prominent opposition figure who was imprisoned in Abu Salim Prison and probably perished in the 1996 massacre, "watching Seif's speech was like watching someone tear off a mask."[22]

Pargeter seems to have it right when she says "Saif Al-Islam increasingly came to replicate his father....just as his father insisted that he had no formal position and was merely the leader of the revolution, so Saif Al-Islam kept repeating that he was simply leader of Libya's civil society."[23] He was, in other words, a modernized version of an arbitrary, capricious and self-absorbed ruler—and the fact that he was the best hope of the reformers did not change that. In many ways, the absence of serious, thorough-going and genuine commitment to political principles among those who, in Chorin's words, "found reformist dialogue profitable or believed it was possible"[24] disabled those same reformers when they were released from their roles in the old regime.

Peter Bartu in Peter Cole and Brian McQuinn's excellent edited volume, *The Libyan Revolution and Its Aftermath*, describes the consequences of unprincipled leadership for the Transitional National Council:

> A shared anxiety throughout the eclectic group of lawyers, academics, former Qadhafi ministers and ambassadors, youth, political prisoners, women, and regional representatives and Qadhafi oppositionists from the diaspora was to show that they had not seized or assumed power. They felt they could claim only to speak and act on behalf of the Libyan people on issues where there was broad consensus.... After forty-two years of Qadhafi, the Libyan opposition, obsessed about legitimate representation, trusted neither themselves nor the outside world...[25]

---

[22] Matar, *The Return: Fathers, Sons and the Land in Between*, 203.

[23] Pargeter, *Libya: The Rise and Fall of Qaddafi*, 208.

[24] Chorin, *Exit the Colonel*, 268.

[25] Bartu, "The Corridor of Uncertainty: The National Transitional Council's Battle for Legitimacy and Recognition," in *The Libyan Revolution and its*

Opposition—and, let it be said, courage—brought these rebels together, but they were not temperamentally rebellious or even particularly assertive; they were modernizers, incrementalists and reformers, who had little experience of open debate about policies and procedures and no common vision of the future. After decades in the shadow of a corrupt and corrupting regime, political compromise too often seemed to mean moral compromise; political choices too often seemed to represent existential decisions. There were few ways to establish and maintain trust in this eclectic group and too many ways to evoke the past to justify special pleading. And in that at least, they were certainly representative: indeed, in many ways they were a microcosm of Libya as a whole.

111

Mistrust: the social fabric of Libya

All the books under review underscore the pathological distrust that characterized Libya in this period. The willingness of ordinary Libyan youth to take extraordinary risks to rid themselves of a cruel and capricious government clearly inspired the older generation that made up the NTC and its allies. But in the willingness of so many young people to put their trust in God and rush into battle was also a devastating testament: there was little else deemed trustworthy. Decades of dissembling, dishonesty and deceit had eroded even the most simple and ordinary civic virtues. Several authors recount the story of the Eshkal brothers as emblematic. Hilsum, for example, tells us that:

> one of the rebel's key assets was General Mohammed Eshkal [also known as Barani Eshkal in some accounts]... whose brigade guarded Bab al Aziziyah and much of central Tripoli. In 1985, during a period of plotting and unrest within the inner circle, Qaddafi had ordered the execution of his brother, Colonel Hassan Eshkal. General Eshkal had quietly nursed his grievance for more than a quarter of a century. He had tried to join the rebels several months earlier but they told him to stay in place until the time came. This [the final siege of Tripoli in August

---

Aftermath, 37.

2011] was that time. Some say he ordered his men to lay down their arms, others that he just disappeared and left them leaderless.[26]

In fact, much of the energy of the rebellion reflected decades of simmering resentment and bitterness; virtually no Libyan family was untouched by the arbitrary and compromising demands of the regime. As Dirk Vandewalle puts in the Cole and McQuinn volume, the Qaddafi regime:

> had systematically destroyed not only the necessary institutions of a modern democratic polity, but also the supporting norms and arrangements—trust in the system, interpersonal trust, the willingness to provide guarantees to those who lose out in political contestations—that sustain democratic systems... The NTC and its backers encountered a low sense of political community and a sauve-qui-peut attitude among Libya's citizens.[27]

Ironically, among the few incubators of trust was prison. As Mary Fitzgerald tells us in her contribution to the Cole and McQuinn volume,

> if anything united Libya's disparate Islamists, it was not so much ideology—beyond a shared and often vaguely formulated wish for government rooted in sharia law—as the bonds formed during incarceration in Abu Slim. Many imprisoned there speak of it as a formative experience, during which ideologies, strategies and tactics were debated.... "Ironically, you could say one year in Abu Slim was worth several on the outside in that we could talk with less fear," recalled Abdullah Shamia, a senior Brotherhood figure who spent eight years in Abu Slim, and later held the economic portfolio in the National

---

[26] Hilsum, *Sandstorm,* 248. Also see Pargeter, *Libya,* 241.

[27] Vandewalle, "Libya's Uncertain Revolution," in *The Libyan Revolution and its Aftermath,* 22.

Transitional Council.[28]

Thus, the protests about Abu Salim were not only the spark that set off
the uprising but also a tacit acknowledgement that prison itself was a
virtually unique site of intellectual ferment and comraderie. Hisham
Matar recounts a conversation with the author and editor Ahmed
Faitori. In 1978, Faitori and other young writers had been invited to a
regime-sponsored book festival; all the participants were then arrested,
most to spend a decade in prison. Faitori reflected: "Qaddafi thought
he was hurting me. Instead, he gave me dozens of writer friends. I now
have a house in every village and town across the country."[29] Fitzgerald
quotes another revolutionary leader: "There were former prisoners in
every Libyan city, with relationships of great trust which created a
strong secure network which grew quickly during the revolution
because it was difficult to disrupt."[30]

If prison was a refuge and an incubator of trust across kin and
region, the very lack of prison time seems to have deprived everyone
else of such attachments. Those incarcerated, if they were not killed,
were left to their own devices for years and they developed deep and
abiding intellectual and emotional ties. Those formally at liberty by
contrast were subject to arbitrary and unpredictable but constant
harassment, physically less painful perhaps but emotionally agonizing:
temptation, surveillance, abuse, enticement, and humiliation. Matar
recounts Saif al-Islam's perennially unfulfilled promises to provide
information about Matar's father as a series of bizarre and excruciating
episodes of hopes raised and dashed. It was almost as if the ordinary
associations of being free and being incarcerated were turned inside
out: perhaps a young dentist from Sirte quoted by Hilsum speaks for
those outside of prison: "we each have Qaddafi inside us, Muammar
killed us, and we think the solution is more killing". [31]

---

[28] Fitzgerald, "Finding Their Place: Libya's Islamists During and After the
Revolution," in *The Libyan Revolution and its Aftermath*, 179.

[29] Matar, *The Return*, 102.

[30] Fitzgerald, "Finding Their Place," 180.

[31] Hilsum, *Sandstorm*, 265.

Blame and Credit: Victory has a thousand fathers

This distrust and appetite for revenge had two particularly deleterious consequences for efforts to organize a polity and government after the collapse of the Qaddafi regime. As Marieke Wierda shows in her essay in the Cole and McQuinn volume, efforts to create an institutional framework for transitional justice were overwhelmed by the complexity of assigning blame:

> Membership in Qadhafi's intricate security web was vast; for instance, Qadhafi's Revolutionary Committees, used to identify and persecute political opponents, number between 60,000 and 100,000. .... A related problem was that many Libyans who may not have participated directly in acts of oppression benefited financially from the former government. A large number, over half a million, were exiled to Tunisia, Egypt and other countries following the revolution. ... The question of who should be punished for which actions (or affiliations) was therefore highly contentious...[32]

In this context, calls to exclude people associated with the Qaddafi regime—"political isolation"—soon trumped "transitional justice." Although the NTC had originally proposed to disqualify only those who, in the Chairman's formulation, had "blood on their hands," by the summer of 2012, the process had become, as Wierda puts it, "more about current political power struggles than addressing the past."[33] Yet by disqualifying all those with any association with the Qaddafi regime, the revolutionaries deprived themselves of virtually all experience of running an administration or managing a country.

The second and related negative consequence of the atmosphere of distrust was a remarkable rivalry over credit for the uprising and its success. Much of this competition was indirect, through symbols and stories of the past. In this, many of the foreign reporters and analysts are often credulous and presumably unwitting accomplices, taking

---

[32] Wierda, "Confronting Qadhafi's Legacy: Transitional Justice in Libya," in *The Libyan Revolution and its Aftermath*, 158.

[33] Wierda, "Confronting Qadhafi's Legacy," 160.

stories of past heroism at face value. Hilsum, for example, tells us uncritically "the 2011 revolution was in part a fight over the legacy of Omar Mukhtar. It was also about reclaiming the heritage of the Sanussi."[34] For some revolutionaries, this was certainly true; the early adoption of the flag of the pre-Qaddafi monarchy as the banner of the revolution by the Benghazi-based NTC was calculated to evoke both the history of resistance in the eastern province and its attachment to the Sanusi Order whose leader had been king. That the Order and the monarchy were far less widely admired in the rest of the country was well known to the revolutionary leaders, of course, but their inclination to inclusiveness was halfhearted. They believed, with some justification, that Benghazi had been particularly poorly treated by Qaddafi. As Pargeter puts it,

> The brutality that the Colonel had employed against the east fostered an extreme resentment... [that] exploded so spectacularly in February 2011, when the east finally took its revenge.[35]

Still, there were other protests, other narratives and other heroes. Pargeter herself observes:

> It was not only in the rebellious east that Libyans were rising up. Al-Zawiya, in the west of the country, came out against the regime on 19 February...The next day clashes broke out in Misarata, where rebels took control of the centre of the city. ...There were uprisings on 18 and 19 February just meters from Qaddafi's Bab Al-Aziziyah residence...[36]

But the early struggles of the capital and western towns were rarely credited in the early days of the uprising. Sean Kane, in the Cole and

---

[34] Hilsum, *Sandstorm*, 19. Hilsum then gives us an error-riddled account of the history of the Sanusiyyah, which is particularly disappointing, given how detailed and accurate so much of the rest of the book is, but Idris did not flee to Egypt "during World War II."

[35] Pargeter, *Libya*, 171.

[36] Pargeter, *Libya*, 223.

McQuinn volume, remarks on the "proprietary eastern feelings over the revolution and a perception that western towns were late to support it" and correctly suggests that "...maintaining a stable Libya will be difficult if its politically hyperactive eastern region does not buy into the new order."[37] But to say, as he does, that "resistance to the Italian occupation, the shaping of the 1951 independence constitution, and most recently, with the 2011 revolution, all emanated from Benghazi"[38] merely exacerbates the regional rivalry. In fact, resistance to (as well as collaboration with) the Italians was widespread across the provinces while the 1951 constitution was engineered by Western powers through the new United Nations. The understandable pride of easterners in their role in modern Libyan history, and in the rebellion itself, need not sanction a wholesale rewriting of that history.

In fact, what Wolfram Lacher and Ahmed Labnouj observe about the Nafusa Mountains in the Cole and McQuinn volume is true of the entire country:

> As over the past century, each mountain town is now writing its own history of the war. The accounts of each community's contribution to the revolution differ sharply from one town to another, as do perceptions of each's involvement with the regime during the war. Downplaying other communities' role has become an integral part of the struggles over the history of the revolution. For Nafusa Mountains communities to overcome the problem of factionalism, they will have to negotiate a common history of the war.[39]

All of Libya will have to negotiate a common history. Hilsum observes that "in Misrata, they were creating their own myth, in which no other Libyans featured" and she reports that "The sole exhibit to be stolen from the Tripoli Museum during the conflict was the possessions of Ramadan Al-Swehli, Misrata's answer to Omar Mukhtar, who had fought against the Italians."[40] McQuinn echoes this worrisome

---

[37] Kane, "Barqa Reborn? Eastern Regionalism and Libya's Political Transition," in *The Libyan Revolution and its Aftermath*, 214, 225.

[38] Kane, "Barqa Reborn?" 226.

[39] Lacher and Labnouj, "Factionalism Resurgent: The War in the Jabal Nafusa," in *The Libyan Revolution and its Aftermath*, 284.

[40] Hilsum, *Sandstorm*, 279.

observation:

> The 17 February Revolution defines modern Misratan identity—domestically as well as internationally. Misrata is now known as the besieged city that survived Qaddafi's onslaught and (perhaps more infamously) captured and killed him. To many Misratans...this was their "manifest destiny," a legacy of [Al-Swehli's] vision for a liberated Libya with Misrata as its nucleus. And it is the legacy of the insurgency against the Italians and their suffering that became an enduring cultural reference in Misrata and Libya more generally.[41]

117

But in fact, the story is more complicated. The resistance to the Italian invasion and occupation was widespread and sustained, and certainly not "wholly-owned" by any locality. So, too, the struggle to recover from the cruelty and negligence of their imperial experience and ultimately to win independence after World War II ended Italian control was hardly unique to a single province or individual. That the Qaddafi regime manipulated the telling of the country's history, appropriating Omar al-Mukhtar as a symbol of the Libyan resistance in part to deprive Cyrenaicans of a local hero, is clear, but it should not excuse further manipulation.

But the story is also complicated because local identities are increasingly mythical attachments. Like Americans who celebrate their "ethnic origins" in places neither they nor their parents have ever seen—the Italy and Ireland of family tradition is long gone—so too Libyans often commemorate attachments to places they hardly know. Hisham Matar's family is from Ajdabiya but he was born in New York and raised in Tripoli; he never lived in the eastern province. McQuinn reports that when asked why protests did not take place in Misrata in the early days of the uprising, he was told "in Misrata, the majority of the people were wealthy, they did not care whether Qadhafi stayed or went, but when [the killing of protestors in Benghazi] happened, everything changed. We all have family in Benghazi. By killing people there, Qadhafi made a mistake; he forced us to choose sides."[42] In fact, as Kane points out, the eastern province, once the home of the most

---

[41] McQuinn, "History's Warriors: The Emergence of Revolutionary Battalions in Misrata," in *The Libyan Revolution and its Aftermath*, 254.

[42] McQuinn, "History's Warriors," 234.

tribal of politics, is no longer so homogenous:

> Eastern Islamists...appeared most established in the parts of the east where the...tribes were not present, notably certain neighborhoods of Benghazi and, especially, the city of Dirna. Major parts of these populaces migrated from Misrata and other western Libyan cities during the mid-twentieth century and thus shared few genealogical ties with the... tribes. Religion—and political Islam specifically—may have therefore become an alternative form of social solidarity and political identity for these migrant families. ... During the revolution itself, these fissures did not fatally undermine the NTC or the civil society that supported it because of their common opposition towards Qadhafi.[43]

Cole and McQuinn argue that the community "narratives are stronger, more distinct and self- contained than one single 'Libyan' narrative. Yet those narrative strands, read together, weave into a single thread that, while discordant, is uniquely 'Libyan.'"[44] That may be true but it is hard to imagine how a tapestry will be woven of these threads if they are not ultimately acknowledged by the Libyans themselves as a shared and collective history. There is much to celebrate in being Libyan—people remarkable for their resilience in the face of adversity and steadfast in their dreams for future generations. Matar reminisces about "the strong years, when my parents had the confident manner of couples that, notwithstanding the usual apprehensions of parents, regard the future as a friendly country."[45]

To restore that confidence, Libyans will have to recall the traditions of heroism that were both selfless and generous. For that, we might give the last word to Hisham Matar's father. When his wife and sons beg him to abandon his work in the opposition, Jaballa Matar admonishes them: "Don't put yourself in competition with Libya. You will always lose."[46] God willing; we can only hope that there are still those who are prepared to sacrifice so that Libya flourishes.

---

[43] Kane, "Barqa Reborn?" 212.

[44] Cole and McQuinn, "Introduction," in *The Libyan Revolution and its Aftermath*, 1.

[45] Matar, *The Return*, 57.

[46] Matar, *The Return*, 38.

What to read

The most academic of these volumes—and in fairness, among the most recent (contributors cite both the Chorin and Hilsum books)—is Peter Cole and Brian McQuinn's edited book, *The Libyan Revolution and Its Aftermath*. For many readers not already familiar with Libya, the descriptions of the street battles in Misrata or the tribal and town alliances in the Jabal Nafusa may be difficult; they are dense and detailed. It is, however, a remarkable collection, uniformly well-informed, intelligent and thoughtful.

For readers more interested in a popular survey, Hilsum's *Sandstorm* is a brisk, engrossing account by a distinguished British journalist who spent time travelling across Libya during the uprising. It includes detailed, eye-witness account of battles between revolutionaries and Qaddafi loyalists. It has only the briefest of "Notes on Sources"—presumably because much of the reporting is her own— but the history is a bit potted, and she could have provided more background references for the curious reader. Pargeter's *Libya* includes such footnotes but its language is distractingly casual and flippant; Qaddafi is repeatedly described as "the ever-proud Bedouin," as if that explains his pathologies, while other Libyan actors are disparaged equally by the too cavalier language: the NTC is described as "a credible bunch."[47]

Forte, Chivvis and Chorin are more concerned with American foreign policy than Libyan politics as such. Forte is more interested in Africa than Libya, more focused on imperialism than revolution. Chivvis appears never to have visited Libya and seems only tangentially interested in the country—he is concerned entirely with "inside the Beltway" Washington maneuvering, about which he seems to provide a credible story. Chorin is evidently quite devoted to the friends he made while serving in Libya and his is the more detailed treatment of US views of the country starting with the resumption of relations in 2003.

Matar's astonishing memoir is written with the sensibility of the novelist he is; it is a beautiful, moving book, conveying in the circumscribed story of one family the history of an entire nation. Chivvis and his colleagues in the Pentagon, as well as everyone who is in a position to make a difference to Libya, should read this book before they do anything more.

---

[47] Pargeter, *Libya*, 239.

What to write

Is it fair to ask for more, after all this? Perhaps not but I would like to see two sets of perspectives better represented.

The first, which foreigners would be well positioned to provide, is about the pebbles that are constantly being thrown in this pool of water, creating ripples that make it difficult to see both the reflections on the surface and the depths below. Who are the international patrons of the warring factions and militias, what is their stake in these proxy wars, why is Libya such an inviting arena for fighting distant battles? For more than a century now, Libya has been a terrain in which Italians and Turks, Egyptians, British and French, Americans and Russians, and now Emiratis and Qataris, have fought—for what? Does the geostrategic value of the land or the country's petroleum really justify this interference?

And, speaking of outside influence, what of the technologies of war? How much of the fighting is fed by apparently limitless supplies of weapons, by digital technologies and media platforms that inflame hatred and deepen mistrust? Were Libyans forced to confront each other without such perverse incitements, would they see themselves together in this pool?

And what might they see? It may be a lot to ask of people who have already been deprived of so much of a decent life, but I wish Libyans would write about themselves. Who might be the Libyan Nelson Mandela or Martin Luther King who will tell us what the upside-down world looked like from the freedom of a Libyan prison under Qaddafi? Who can write about life as teenagers in the Nafusa Mountains, the Misrata markets, Sabha and Ajadabiya and Baida? Who will write the love stories, the family histories, the accounts of everyday life—the gossip, the weather, the childhood adventures and old people's reminiscences? Once Libyans can record ordinary life, they may be able to reclaim it, and we will all be able to see past our reflections and beneath the surface of this pool of too troubled water.

AFIFA LTIFI

Review of The Slave Pens by Najwa Bin Shatwan (Beirut: Dār al-Sāqī, 2016)

SINCE ITS PUBLICATION IN 2016, Najwa Bin Shatwan's *The Slave Pens* (Arabic: زرايب العبيد) has been garnering acclaim by literati across the Arabophone world. Shortlisted for the 2017 International Prize for Arabic Fiction,[1] it had been hailed as one of the Libyan author's must-translate recent works. Originally penned in Arabic, for several years only an excerpt of the novel had been translated into English.[2] Before writing *The Slave Pens*, Bin Shatwan had published two novels, *Orange Content* (2008) and *The Horse Hairs* (2007), with the latter earning her the Sudanese al-Bagrawiya Festival prize. In 2009, Bin Shatwan was listed among the 39 best Arab authors under the age of 40 by the Beirut39 Project for her short story "The Pool and the Piano," which was featured in their anthology. Her short story "Return Ticket" has recently been featured in *Banthology: Stories from Unwanted Nations* (2018), an anthology of creative writing from the seven countries of the so-called Muslim Ban.

The Slave Pens resurrects the fading memory of slavery in early 20th-century Ottoman Libya. Via incessant flashbacks experienced by the narrators 'Atiqa and Ali, the novel enters the many lives of those displaced from more southern parts of Africa to end up at the service of those on the northern shores of the continent. It delves into the microhistories of the enslaved and pays special attention to that which pertains to the interiority of the black enslaved women of the period. Akin to the decimated memory of trans-Saharan slavery, Bin Shatwan recounts their stories of enslavement and its afterlife in fragments,

---

[1] https://www.arabicfiction.org/en/2017-shortlist-announced

[2] Sawad Hussein and Marcia Lynx Qualey, "An Excerpt from Najwa Bin Shatwan's International Prize for Arabic Fiction-shortlisted 'Slave Pens'", https://arablit.org/2017/07/10/an-excerpt-from-najwa-bin-shatwans-international-prize-for-arabic-fiction-shortlisted-slave-pens/. The novel has now been translated into English in its entirety and published as *The Slave Yards* (Syracuse University Press, 2020), translated by Nancy Roberts. Note that this review applies only to the original, Arabic text.

shedding light on the socioeconomic realities that inform the limited dynamism of their social statuses oscillating between servitude, concubinage, and prostitution.

The story follows the life of the enslaved black woman Ta'widha and Muhammad Bin Shatwan, a Libyan who owns her and takes her as a concubine in addition to his wife. As Muhammad goes off on a trade trip, his family marries Ta'widha off to another slave, kills her son, and disappears her in the city's brothel. Ta'widha later manages to escape the brothel and starts a new life on the outskirts of Benghazi in an area called al-Ṣābrī, where she gives birth to another child fathered by Muhammad, 'Atiqa, whom she raises along with an adoptive son, Miftah.

As Ta'widha's life events unfold, we are exposed to the grotesque normalization of slaves' disposability and objectification as means of transactions. They are enumerated among cargos of "salt" and "flour" as their lives swing between arbitrariness and necessity. The chronicles of Ta'widha's life under slavery show the entrapment of the slave body in the state of exception under the biopolitical regime of the period. Although preserved as a domestic and a pleasure concubine, she is immediately sacrificed through the many attempts of Muhammad's family to send her to the slave market, marry her off to another slave, and ultimately disappear her beyond the reach of their son. Ta'widha's acceptance of her role in the libidinal economy of slavery does not shield her from being reduced to a bare life, where for the preservation of the normative relationship of Muhammad and his "honorable" wife, she is made yet again disposable on the auction podium. The numerous forced abortions on Ta'widha's body, enacted mostly without her knowledge, show not only her lack of agency but also the fungibility[3] of both black and master-slave offspring.

One does not need to explore scenes of subjugation to imagine the gravity of the institution of slavery, but the novel provides a shaking reminder about the depressing lives of slaves, especially women. As Ta'widha endures the slave auction, standing bare-breasted, we are given a glimpse into the severity of her condition. Unlike the prevalent assumption that renders Islamic slavery benign and pits it against chattel and plantation-model slavery, the novel proves the extent to which slave lives and bodies were abused in the precarious domestic

---

[3] In Agamben's sense; see Giorgio Agamben, *Homo Sacer. Sovereign Power and Bare Life* (Stanford University Press, 1998).

realm. Islamic jurisdiction and the social norms that observe it remain silent in the face of injustices enacted on the enslaved woman.

The novel equally complicates our understanding of the processes of liberation granted to enslaved women who bear masters' children. The child that Taʻwidha bears from Muhammad does not redeem her from her enslaved status nor become her winning ticket to freedom. Unlike some female slaves incorporated into the concubinage system, Taʻwidha fails to thrive as a concubine with *umm al-walad* status (i.e. a slave who had borne her master a child and was therefore to be freed upon his death). The assumption that freedom is automatically granted to the enslaved woman after birthing mixed offspring is revealed to be a complicated process that does not easily apply to everyone. The love of the master does not elevate Taʻwidha beyond the position of the concubine but instead further criminalizes her as a superstitious black slave. As Muhammad develops strong emotional ties to her, his feelings are discredited by his family and attributed to the effects of the black magic that his concubine is accused of mastering.

In an interview with BBC Arabic,[4] Bin Shatwan underscored the role of oral history and collective memory in helping her reimagine the stories of the long-silenced enslaved subjects of the period. Biased as it is, the reliance on such selective collective memory leaves indelible marks on this work of fiction. It becomes apparent throughout the chapters that the author does not rest on a robust written historical repository. Throughout the novel, she rarely uses periodization or hints at political events that would inform the reader about the historical time period in which it is set. Echoing the dearth of historical literature on slavery, the novel only succeeds at capturing the feel of a hazy history, as it is collectively sensed and remembered. Although a historian by training,[5] Bin Shatwan preferred to simulate the storyline as retained in the collective reminiscence and rehearsed from generation to generation, going back and forth with her inventive memory without adopting a sequential narrative line.[6] The only instance where we are given a temporal sense of the events is when Bin Shatwan mentions the

---

[4] "عالم الكتاب: "زرايب العبيد" وتراث الرق" (BBC Arabic, July 8, 2017), at http://www.bbc.com/arabic/tv-and-radio-40543199.

[5] Bin Shatwan obtained a doctoral degree in the history of Ottoman Libya from the Sapienza Università di Roma in 2017.

[6] See her talk given at the Abu Dhabi International Book Fair in 2017, https://www.youtube.com/watch?v=HvvoAjghapY.

Italian mission and the Sanussi brotherhood, hinting at the centrality of the Sanussi order to slavery in Libya.

The novel raises many urgent questions about the legal conditions of the characters and the milieu they inhabit. One might ask, were they runaway slaves or manumitted? If free, how were they ejected from the institution of slavery, especially since the novel's events unfold before the abolition of slavery in Libya. Even as she situates the story at the marginal slave pens of Benghazi, the author does not give any allusion to the context of the establishment of these peripheral slums. It is worth mentioning that the slave pens (زرايب العبيد) of the book's title are not fictional. These animal pen-like shelters actually existed in Ottoman Benghazi. according to the Benghazi-born author. In the above-mentioned interview, she reveals that she stumbled upon a photograph of them, allegedly taken by an unknown Italian traveler before the Italian occupation of Libya, on a friend's desk. In it, three black women appear standing beside their ravaged huts along with a little child. The four black subjects of the photograph gripped the writer and inspired her to investigate the "slave pens" and, ultimately, write the novel.

The uncritical use of terminology remains an undeniable flaw that the novelist ought to have rectified. Bin Shatwan uses the term "Africa" to refer to the land of origin of the enslaved characters in the novel. Referring to the sub-Saharan side with the historically loaded and undifferentiated term "Africa" shows the extent to which the novelist is, herself, perpetuating the dismemberment of Libya and North Africa from the rest of the continent. The use of slurs and terms to refer to black characters is equally problematic. The epithets used by 'Atiqa, Ta'widha's daughter, in describing the variations and shades of blackness of some characters come across as if the narrator is not black herself. In this way, the novel seems to fluctuate between 'Atiqa's voice and the omniscient Bin Shatwan, whose views, curiosity, and lack of knowledge about these identities slip into 'Atiqa's voice. Terms like *zanjī* (زنجي), *shūshān* (شوشان), *'abd* (عبد), and *khādim* (خادم) seem to be interchangeable with the color black, which in itself is synonymous with the status of servitude. As she names her characters, the writer does little to illuminate the meanings of their names, either. 'Atiqa's name (عتيقة), for instance, literally means "freed slave" and yet the novelist does not reveal enough about the reason behind which the mother, Ta'widha, would name her daughter as such. Why would Ta'widha choose to burden her daughter with a name of such problematic connotation? The author's choice of Muhammad's surname, Bin Shatwan, remains equally curious as it is the novelist's own surname. Why did Najwa

Bin Shatwan burden herself with such a responsibility vis-à-vis her characters? When asked about this choice, she said that she did not want to "clash with people's real-life sensitivities" by invoking another Libyan family's last name.[7] But in a work where race and color take center stage, it is baffling that the novelist does little to illuminate the meanings, histories and reasons behind which these terms and names are chosen. As the omniscient narrator's voice interrupts both 'Atiqa's and Ali's streams of consciousness throughout the novel, Bin Shatwan's choice of lending her last name to the slaveholding family prompts more questions about the genre of the novel and the extent to which it holds the seeds of an autobiographical text.

Despite these deliberately overlooked deficiencies, the novelist's bravery in tackling the taboo subject of slavery remains laudable. Albeit fictional, the novel is the first of its kind in attempting to recollect, imagine, and incarnate the female enslaved figure. Generally, the question of gender in relation to slavery has rarely been broached in North African novels. Notable exceptions are Fatima Mernissi's *Dreams of Trespass* (1994), Taher Ben Jelloun's *Moha le fou, Moha le sage* (1978), and Abdelkrim Ghallab's دفنّا الماضي (*We buried the past*, 1968), in which the subject was only timidly alluded to. *The Slave Pens* is thus arguably only the second North African historical novel which centers on the black enslaved subject, after Tunisian writer Béchir Khraïef's برق الليل (*L'éclair de la nuit*, 1961).

The lack of slave narratives from the period of trans-Saharan slavery renders the task of reincarnating the silenced challenging. It is only through fictitious recollections of these fading memories that one can capture the feel of history and come up with what might simulate lost archival testimonies. In this recovery of this buried history, the Libyan writer spectacularly reincarnates the black enslaved woman who, in the words of historian Chouki El Hamel, is "the tragic heroine of North African slavery."[8]

---

[7] "Confronting A Darker Chapter" (Qantara.de, 5 May 2017), at https://en.qantara.de/content/libyan-author-najwa-binshatwan-on-the-slave-pens-confronting-a-dark-chapter

[8] Chouki El Hamel, *Black Morocco: a History of Slavery, Race, and Islam* (Cambridge University Press, 2013), 11.

Najat Abdulhaq

127

Review of Jewish Libya: Memory & Identity in Text & Image, *edited by Jacques Roumani, David Meghnagi, & Judith Roumani (New York: Syracuse University Press, 2018)*

Middle eastern and north african religious minorities, in particular Jewish communities, have attracted distinguished scholarly interest in the last several years. The Jews of Libya have been on the margins of this interest compared to other Jewish communities in the region, and remain absent in several anthologies on North African and Middle Eastern Jews.[1] Nevertheless, a few works on Jewish Libyans in particular have been published in the last few decades, including Italian historian Renzo De Felice's *Jews in Arab Land, Libya: 1835-1970,*[2] Rachael Simon's specialized studies of Jewish Libyan women such as *Change within Tradition among Jewish Women in Libya,*[3] or Harvey Goldberg's *Jewish Life in Muslim Libya: Rivals and Relatives.*[4] Other works have focused on the distinctive Arabic dialect of the Jews in Tripoli.[5]

---

[1]   Compare, for example, Reeva Spector Simon, Michael Menachem Laskier, and Sara Reguer (eds.), *The Jews of the Middle East and North Africa in Modern Times* (New York: Columbia University Press, 2003) or Emily Gottreich and Daniel J. Schroeter (eds.), *Jewish Culture and Society in North Africa* (Bloomington: Indiana University Press, 2011).

[2]   Renzo De Felice, *Ebrei in un paese arabo: Gli ebrei nella Libia contemporanea tra colonialismo, nazionalismo arabo e sionismo (1835-1970)* (Bologna: Il Mulino, 1978). Translated by Judith Roumani as *Jews in Arab Land, Libya: 1835-1970* (Austin: University of Texas Press, 1985).

[3]   Rachel Simon, *Change within Tradition among Jewish Women in Libya* (Seattle: University of Washington Press, 1992).

[4]   Harvey Goldberg, *Jewish Life in Muslim Libya: Rivals and Relatives* (Chicago: University of Chicago Press, 1990).

[5]   Sumikazu Yoda, *The Arabic Dialect of the Jews of Tripoli (Libya): Grammar,*

Abdulhaq

128

Despite these important works, the presence of Libya's Jews in scholarship and in the consciousness of scholars of the Arab and Islamic worlds is far less than that of the Jewish communities in Egypt or Morocco. It is within this context of scholarship that the importance of the volume under review is made clear and offers an important voice for Libyan Jews, marking a beginning to the end of their absence in existing scholarship.

Jewish Libya: Memory & Identity in Text & Image is interdisciplinary and comprehensive. The edited volume offers a very good overview of Libyan Jewish history, contemporary life, customs, food/culinary arts, and literature. In addition, there is a specific part devoted to the discussion of women, which is not common in many works discussing Middle Eastern and North African Jewish communities. In particular, the chapters on culinary arts, food, and wedding traditions, alongside the personal interviews demonstrate how the Jewish community was interwoven with larger Libyan society; Jewish traditions were an integral part of everyday life in Libya.

The volume is composed of thirteen contributions written by eleven scholars, the majority of whom possess a Libyan background, which offers an added authenticity of the work. Others, like Japanese linguist Sumikazu Yoda, are specialists in their field and present unique work pertaining to Jews of Libya. The volume is an anthology that is conceptualized for non-specialist readers to have a contextual understanding, as the editors write in the introduction. This work is a reflection of the complex and diverse structures and multiple identities of North African societies, where one-dimensional or nationalist perspectives are not able to grasp this diversity.

The book addresses well the impact of colonial and postcolonial history for Jewish communities in Libya. The Italian colonial era had contradictory influences on the Jewish community. The era fostered education for the community at the beginning of the century and integration with Italian Jews, which influenced the community to depart from the intellectual and physical walls of the *ḥāra*, the Jewish quarter. In 1943, however, Italian colonial rule was responsible for detaining 2600 members of the Jewish community—of whom 562 died—in Jadu (Italian spelling Giado) on Mussolini's orders, under the

---

Text and Glossary (Wiesbaden: Harrassowitz, 2005).

suspicion of sympathizing with the enemy. Furthermore, fascist Italian authorities deported 300 Jews to Germany and it was British passports that rescued them from death in the German concentration camps.

Those who influenced the modernizing of the community at the beginning of the century were also those who detained them during the war and turned the anger of the Muslim majority against Libyan Jews in 1945 and 1948. The masses that were mobilized against their Jewish compatriots connected them to the colonial power, the war and, later in 1948, to Israel. This reflects the transition that Libyan society, and those of neighboring countries, underwent throughout the twenty-five-year period between 1943 and 1967, influenced by World War II, anti-colonial movements, the establishment of Israel, and the rise of nationalism. Europe continues to reflect on its own experience of World War II, particularly the Holocaust, and its Jewish communities in Europe, often overlooking the direct and indirect influence of these events on the Jewish communities south of the Mediterranean.[6] The strength of this edited volume, among many others, is its focus on this particular aspect of European history during World War II in connection to Libyan Jewish communities.

Another distinctive feature of this anthology is its dedicated discussion of literature, which is unique compared to other comprehensive works on the Jews of North Africa or the Middle East. Literature and autobiographies, not classical historical sources, have a cardinal role—much more than is regularly acknowledged—in being an important source of micro-history and insight into daily life, including the emotions associated with, and context of, political events impacting Jewish communities in Libya.

Jewish Libya represents a scholarly enrichment to existing studies of pre-1948 Jewish history in North Africa and the Middle East. These strengths notwithstanding, a critique needs to be addressed: the contributions in some chapters are anecdotal and the descriptive style sometimes lacks a solid research and theoretical framework. Other chapters are primarily summaries of other works. This is useful for interested readers but not necessary for specialized scholars. In addition, the authors emphasize in the introduction the rejection

---

[6] See Aomar Boum and Sarah Abrevaya Stein (eds.), *The Holocaust and North Africa* (Stanford: Stanford University Press, 2018).

of the "Arabness" of Libya and the "non-Arabness" of its Jews. This focus neglects a debate, though not as wide, about pan-Arabism and Arab nationalism in the histories of North Africa. Going into a more detailed discussion about these approaches and debating them would have given the work more solid theoretical ground.[7] A final comment concerns the use of terminology in parts of the work. In Part One, on the history of the first centuries, the author uses the term "Eretz Yisrael," not only a Biblical term but one associated with a particular ideology—one would expect the use of terms that reflect a modern political, and less ideological, understanding.

---

[7]   See the work of Israeli sociologist and critical theorist Yehouda Shenhav, mainly *The Arab Jews: A Postcolonial Reading of Nationalism, Religion, and History* (Stanford: Stanford University Press, 2006), in which he rejects the one-dimensional analysis of the history of the Jews in pre-1948 Middle East and North Africa and criticizes the official Israeli narrative and handling of this history. Shenhav is part of a wider approach among Jewish and non-Jewish scholars on this question.

www.ingramcontent.com/pod-product-compliance
Lightning Source LLC
Chambersburg PA
CBHW050655270326
41927CB00012B/3035